Inter

Interpreting Shakespeare on Screen

Deborah Cartmell

© Deborah Cartmell 2000

First published 2000 by
MACMILLAN PRESS LTD
Houndmills, Basingstoke, Hampshire RG21 6XS
and London
Companies and representatives throughout the world

ISBN 0–333–65211–8 hardcover
ISBN 0–333–65212–6 paperback

A catalogue record for this book is available
from the British Library.

This book is printed on paper suitable for recycling and
made from fully managed and sustained forest sources

10   9   8   7   6   5   4   3   2   1
09 08 07 06 05 04 03 02 01 00

Printed in Hong Kong

To Hester, Jake and Ian Bradley and in memory
of Roy and Jayne Cartmell

Contents

Preface

This book considers screen adaptations of Shakespeare's dramas as interpretations of Shakespeare's plays as well as interpreting the place of Shakespeare on screen within the classroom and within the curriculum. My aim is to consider ways of studying Shakespeare on screen which need not be director- or play-centred, or even 'Shakespeare-centred'; in fact an analysis of films of the plays, on more than one level, tends to reduce Shakespeare to the position of co-screenwriter. In a newspaper review, Mark Lawson has noted that there have been three distinct waves of Shakespeare on screen – the 1940s, the 1960s and the 1990s;[1] and how Shakespeare is used in film and television in these three distinct periods, focusing on the representations of violence (Chapter 1: *Macbeth* and *King Lear*), gender (Chapter 2: *Hamlet*), sexuality (Chapter 3: *Romeo and Juliet* and *Much Ado About Nothing*), race (Chapter 4: *Othello* and *The Tempest*) and nationalism (Chapter 5: *Henry V*) is the concern of this book.

The first chapter, through an examination of the representation of violence in screen adaptations of Shakespeare's plays, considers what is at stake in translating Shakespeare to screen. The second chapter, through a consideration of representations of gender in film versions of *Hamlet*, charts the growth of the Shakespeare-on-screen industry. The following chapters consider the developing and shifting representations of sexuality, race and nationalism in various film adaptations and inevitably challenge the presumed stability of the Shakespearean text itself. The examination of Shakespeare on screen raises questions about the relationship between past and present and high and low culture and, far from the 'dumbing down' of Shakespeare (and, by implication, English literature), it allows us to move beyond the formal boundaries of institutional English and explore the growing interface between English and Media Studies.

The soundtracks of parts of Franco Zeffirelli's *Romeo and Juliet*

(1968), Kenneth Branagh's *Much Ado About Nothing* (1993), Baz
Luhrmann's *William Shakespeare's Romeo + Juliet,* Orson Welles's
Othello (1952) and Oliver Parker's *Othello* (1995) are juxtaposed with
play texts in Chapters 3 and 4 in order to demonstrate how different
directors/writers select and change the texts for their own purposes.
Identifying and explaining what is left out can be illuminating for an
understanding of how Shakespeare is manufactured on screen.
Students are often amazed to discover that the most interesting bits
are often missing from the film texts, and this raises awareness of just
how Shakespeare is 'popularised', that is, 'spin-doctored' for popular
consumption. It is hoped that readers will construct their own
play/film texts as a starting point for analysing screen texts of
Shakespeare.

It is virtually impossible to keep up to date with developments in
Shakespeare on screen, given, as film reviewer Jonathan Coe
complains in *New Statesman* (1997), there seems to be no end to
them:

> In the past few months I've done nothing but re-read classic novels
> and plays. My desk groans under the weight of Cole's Notes and old
> school essays, as I desperately refamiliarise myself with Hardy, Jane
> Austen, and, of course, William Shakespeare, every one of whose
> plays seems to have been filmed at least twice this year.[2]

Unfortunately, some of the best adaptations of Shakespeare on screen
are not easy to obtain and accordingly, this analysis focuses on 'main-
stream', easily accessible televisual and film adaptations, so as to be
'user-friendly', or of maximum use for students and teachers. Indeed,
it is difficult to draw a line between what is an adaptation and what is
not. Although, for practical reasons, this study focuses largely on
'straight' adaptations, it also touches on looser ones. A tentative
taxonomy can be constructed of the various types of adaptation,
based on Geoffrey Wagner's division of screen adaptations of novels
into 'transposition', 'commentary' and 'analogy'. 'Transposition'
adapts the text as accurately as possible (Kenneth Branagh's *Hamlet*
of 1996, for example), 'commentary' alters the original (such as Baz
Luhrmann's *William Shakespeare's Romeo + Juliet* (1996), which
rearranges the lines and changes the ending) and 'analogy' uses the
original text as a point of departure (for example, John Madden's

Acknowledgements

I would like to thank Pluto Press and Lawrence & Wishart for allowing me to extend earlier discussions of *Henry V* ('The Henry V Flashback: Kenneth Branagh's Shakespeare', in *Pulping Fictions: Consuming Culture Across the Literature/Media Divide*, ed. Deborah Cartmell, Ian Hunter, Heidi Kaye and Imelda Whelehan (London: Pluto, 1996)); Imelda Whelehan and Deborah Cartmell, 'Through a Painted Curtain: Laurence Olivier's Henry V', in *War Culture: Social Change and Changing Experience in World War Two*, ed. Pat Kirkham and David Thoms (London: Lawrence & Wishart, 1995); and *The Shakespeare Yearbook*, where an earlier part of Chapter 2 initially appeared (1997). Thanks are also due to my students for allowing me to reproduce their work in Appendix 1. Finally I wish to thank De Montfort University for allowing me the time to complete this project and for giving me the opportunity to teach Shakespeare on screen.

1 Shakespeare, Film and Violence: Doing Violence to Shakespeare

Introduction

Most studies of adaptation confine themselves to the novel, alerting us to the ways in which the nineteenth-century realist novel, especially, lends itself to cinematic reworking.[1] Shakespeare on screen is normally considered on its own, without comparison to other literary adaptations, usually play-, director-, or film-centred.

The adaptation of the novel is more easily explained than the adaptation of Shakespeare. As the nineteenth-century novel paved the way, in part, for cinematic devices in the early twentieth century, the modernist novel borrowed from cinema, drawing attention to its filmic encoding processes. Writing, such as that of Virginia Woolf in the early twentieth century, undoubtedly shows the influence of the cinema in its translation of cinematic devices, such as zooms, close-ups, change of focus, flashbacks, dissolves and tracking shots, into literary equivalents.[2] Sergei Eisenstein's famous essay, 'Dickens, Griffith and the Film Today', shows how Griffith's montage techniques employ close-up details in imitation of Dickens's narratives.[3] As film provided inspiration for the novelist, the novel, especially the nineteenth-century realist novel, was remarkably 'filmic' in its ability to transport the reader into a self-contained fictional world. Shakespeare, on the other hand, seems a peculiar choice for film.

Yet Shakespeare seems equally adaptable to cinema; many would agree with Laurence Olivier, who has repeatedly implied that Shakespeare would have written films, if only he had the chance. There may be some truth in his statement in his Foreword to '*Hamlet*': *The Film and the Play* (1948) that 'Nothing that we know of

Shakepeare suggests that he actually enjoyed being "cabin'd, cribb'd, confined" by the rudimentary conditions of the stage for which he wrote.'[4] Arguably, today, Shakespeare is known to teenagers as a screenwriter first and as a dramatist second, as an American television narrator concluded in a programme on Shakespeare studies: 'Shakespeare is now Hollywood's hottest screenplay writer.'[5] The adaptation of Shakespeare, perhaps more than any other writer, inspires the fidelity debate and divides those who perceive the text as sacred and/or 'timeless' from those who see the text as an unstable entity which is best when freely adapted.

As Harriet Hawkins has demonstrated, there is no end to adaptations of Shakespeare, and perhaps 'Shakespeare's plays would necessarily have to be required reading for practically any course in the historical origins of popular modern genres.'[6] In other words, Shakespeare's plays are embedded in a host of popular forms:

> 'Come to my bed', says Angelo to Isabella, 'or I'll have your brother killed.' 'Come to my bed', said J.R. to Sue Ellen in Dallas, 'or I'll have your innocent young lover jailed on a drug charge.'[7]

But this is Shakespeare without words – or the structure without the content. The question we need to ask, is if we lose the words do we lose 'Shakespeare'? What distinguishes Shakespeare on screen from Shakespeare in the theatre, or Shakespeare on the page, according to Alan Dent, writing on Olivier's film of *Hamlet* in 1948, is that one appeals to the eyes, the other to the ears:

> The whole technique of the stage . . . is built on the fact that the ear, and therefore eventually the mind, are the things to be gratified and interested. What we see – or *can* see – in the theatre is, although important, much less important by comparison. What we hear is what matters.[8]

But we still haven't answered the question: why film Shakespeare? Films of Shakespeare's plays are different from adaptations of eighteenth- or nineteenth-century novels in that their success cannot be attributed to a nostalgic recreation of an age gone by; they are often set in different, even contemporary periods.[9] Harriet Hawkins partially answers this question of why Shakespeare films have been so marketable by explaining how the narrative structures of Shakespeare's plays lend themselves to popular forms; that is, the stories can be modernised or updated. Films of Shakespeare's plays are not escapist representations of an idyllic past in the same way that films of Jane Austen's novels can be. The need to 'concretise', to make the text 'more real', may be another reason for adapting Shakespeare to film.[10] This may be part of the attraction behind the popular *Shakespeare in Love* (John Madden, 1998) which provides us with visualisations of the Rose Theatre, Philip Henslowe, Richard Burbage, Christopher Marlowe and the young John Webster, not to mention Shakespeare himself. But it is becoming increasingly the case that viewers have no prior knowledge of the text or its context and therefore nothing to make concrete; clearly there is an audience who will go to a film in order to see what a particular director made it look like, but there is also an audience who go to a film, wanting to see, for the first time, what Shakespeare is like. Another reason why adaptations of classic literature have proved so successful is that they provide the viewer with what French sociologist Pierre Bourdieu has described as 'cultural capital',[11] in this case, a quick and easy way to become 'cultured'. In their study of Vitagraph Pictures' 'quality' films, produced between 1907 and 1913, William Uricchio and Roberta Pearson have argued how 'engagement with certain cultural commodities' 'distinguish the participating subject from other members of social formations'.[12] Adaptations of Shakespeare and Dante, for example – 'films deluxe' – capitalised on bringing 'moral edification' and/or 'culture' to the barely literate masses. This, it seems to me, is the reason behind the continued success of Shakespeare on film. Even though the adaptation may be a watered-down version of the original it is, somehow, culturally consecrated: we still come away with something special, something 'Shakespearean'. There is embedded in our culture an almost religious need for Shakespeare, typified by comments such as those by Wilson Knight writing in the midst of World War II: 'we need expect no Messiah, but we might, at this hour, turn to Shakespeare, a national prophet if ever there was one, concerned deeply with the royal soul of England'.[13] What better way to spread the word than through film? This seems to be the aim of Kenneth Branagh, whose introduction to the screenplay of *Hamlet* (1996) reads like a conversion narrative. His first encounter with the play was a 'road to Damascus' experience:

I felt I had encountered a genuine force of nature, and that journey home and for sometime afterwards, its memory made me glad to be alive. But then I was fifteen.

Nevertheless . . . I believe that much of what has followed in my life was affected by that experience.[14]

Certainly the desire to convert others is the declared mission of those directors who loom largely in the Shakespeare-on-screen canon: Laurence Olivier, Franco Zeffirelli and Kenneth Branagh, who span the 'three ages' of Shakespeare on screen, that is, the 1940s, 1960s and 1990s.

Conversion to Shakespeare has itself become a popular cultural narrative; witness heart-warming family sitcoms or films such as *Dead Poets' Society* (1989, directed by Peter Weir). An extremely common popular narrative is one in which a child resists reading or performing Shakespeare until he or she finally 'sees the light' and is liberated into a much more meaningful world. This mission – as well as the audience's desire to be converted – is the subtext or the covert agenda of many films of Shakespeare. This conversion-to-Shakespeare narrative is ingeniously satirised in *The Last Action Hero* (1993, directed by John McTiernan). A schoolteacher, played by Joan Plowright (herself Mrs Laurence Olivier), shows a clip from Olivier's *Hamlet*. Her eleven-year-old pupil, bored by Hamlet's inertia, transforms Hamlet into his action-man hero, played by Arnold Schwarzenegger. This is a Hamlet who knows the answer to the question, 'to be, or not to be'; 'not to be', he emphatically answers himself, tossing a grenade over his shoulder, nonchalantly blowing up the castle behind him. The film cuts to the boy watching a cartoon, suggesting how far we have come from *Hamlet*. In a similar way, an adaptation's radical departure from the source is provocatively announced in *Clueless* (1995), Amy Heckerling's 'free' adaptation of Jane Austen's *Emma*, where the implication is that even a diluted and trivialised *Emma* – like the out-of-context quotations from Shakespeare and Dickens in the film – is better than no *Emma* at all. Cher's/Emma's unlikely correction of a more 'cultured' girl's misattribution of 'To thine own self be true' to Hamlet instead of Polonius (Cher informs us that she might not know *Hamlet*, but she does know Mel Gibson) is, in many ways, the moral of the film. Cher has gained some useful 'cultural capital', thanks to Mel Gibson's *Hamlet*.

This book will concentrate on how and why Shakespeare is appropriated in popular films; but rather than concentrating on specific texts or directors, it looks at how Shakespeare is used by the film industry to appeal to the masses in terms of the presentation of issues such as gender, sexuality, race, violence and nationalism. In order to do this, it is necessary to negotiate the differences (as far as it's possible to do so) between the original conditions of the drama's production and those of the film's construction. Although the texts are, undeniably, appropriated for educational purposes in many cinematic reconstructions, these interestingly coincide with Hollywood ideology which, as James Monaco has described, is, in spite of the revolutionary form of film, fundamentally conservative:

> Thus, two paradoxes control the poetics of film, on the one hand, the form of film is revolutionary, on the other, the content is most often conservative of traditional values.[15]

Shakespeare on film, at least for those who maintain that the dramatist is a spokesman for reactionary ideology, seems ideally suited for Hollywood adaptations, best borne out by the number of Shakespeare films claiming various degrees of fidelity.

A film or televisual adaptation can be distinguished from a play, as Luke McKernan has usefully noted: 'a play is a text which may be performed on a stage, but a film is both text and performance'.[16] When reading Shakespeare on screen, it is crucial that we distinguish the text from the adaptation in such a way as we separate story from plot,[17] or stories told versus stories presented. The story (the play text) consists of the basic raw materials, whereas the plot (the film) is the way in which the story is constructed or creatively reshaped. The film can be examined in terms of its spatial and aural organisation, in which we are provided with a series of codes which manipulate our reaction to the source story. It is important to note that a film is not simply an adaptation of a play; the play is only one element of its intertextuality. Nonetheless, the source story (the play by Shakespeare) is interpreted through a number of cinematic and 'extra-cinematic' codes. These have been usefully suggested by Brian McFarlane, who attempts to avoid questions of value judgements or authenticity by 'scientifically' comparing narrative strategies:

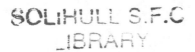

> cinematic codes: we come to know that 'fade out/fade in' announces
> a passage of time; a 'cut' indicates a change in narrative direction,
> blurred focus prepares us for a flashback or dream sequence
> language codes – for example, accents, tones
> visual codes – dress, colour, set, what is selected for viewing
> non linguistic codes – music, background noises
> cultural codes – set, historical, national, religious signifiers[18]

Although the words of the Shakespearean text may be retained in a film adaptation, film adds another 'language' to the text. Cinematic codes provide a filmic shorthand and are useful in reducing vast chunks of text. As Virginia Woolf observed, cinema has 'within its grasp innumerable symbols for emotions that so far failed to find expression' in literature.[19] These codes both compete with and replace the words of the source texts.

Language codes – how people speak, whether they are American or British, loud or quiet – invariably influence our perception. The mixture of American and British actors in a Shakespeare film, for example, has a different effect than a purely British production. Kenneth Branagh's *Henry V* (1989) is not an obvious Hollywood-styled production as its main cast consists solely of British actors. Adaptations of 'classic novels' tend to bear a British stamp of approval and, as such, distance themselves from Hollywood productions where we are accustomed to the British being the villains and the Americans, the heroes.[20] The mixing of accents in Branagh's *Much Ado About Nothing* (1993) and *Hamlet* or Parker's *Othello* (1995), undoubtedly with an eye to the lucrative American market, makes Shakespeare appear more 'universal' and less British, and thus alters our perception of nationalism in Shakespeare. Nonetheless, the more mixed the accents, the less 'authentic' these adaptations appear. Branagh cunningly gets round the problem in *Hamlet* by assigning cameo roles to American stars while retaining a mainly British cast.

Visual codes provide us with another layer of text to take into account when evaluating an adaptation. Laurence Olivier's English troops in *Henry V* (1944) shoot their arrows at the charging French army from left to right (the enemies – the French – moving from right to left). Left to right is a movement pleasing and 'natural' to the Western eye (as we tend to read a film, like a book, from left to right) and therefore implicitly sanctified as the right way. Elizabeth Taylor as

Kate in Zeffirelli's *Taming of the Shrew* (1967) gazes lovingly at Richard Burton's Petruchio through a keyhole – we instantly know, in spite of what she says, that she's playing hard to get. This radically reshapes our reading of the text from one which potentially challenges and exposes the subjugation of women into a play about a woman who secretly wants to be tamed. The colour of the actor, similarly, can influence our reading. Denzel Washington's Don John's proposal (or however you interpret, 'Will you have me, lady?')[21] to Emma Thompson's Beatrice in *Much Ado About Nothing* is more noticeable and problematic than it would be if the two actors were the same colour. Beatrice's refusal, no doubt accidentally, can be interpreted as racist; a reading which is obviously not present in the play text.

Non-linguistic sounds – the most obvious of these being music – can influence our perception of the written text. Kenneth Branagh has *Non nobis* sung at the end of the Battle of Agincourt in a manner to suggest that it is not a song of regret and mourning, but one of triumph that will raise the spirits. The film-maker (not Shakespeare) manoeuvres a reading which ultimately applauds rather than condemns Henry's war. Similarly, in *Much Ado About Nothing*, Branagh begins with the song 'Sigh no more Ladies, sigh no more/ Men were deceivers ever' spoken by Beatrice, implying that she is, from the first, aware of the injustices of men to women. In the play text, it is sung once by Balthasar to the men (II.iii.61) which is included in Branagh's film. Yet Patrick Doyle's musical arrangement of the piece, used throughout the film, takes away the bitter edge of the verse, and in the closing sequence, the song seems to lose the words altogether and stands as a triumphant celebration of the equality of the men and women within their relationships.

Finally, cultural codes, such as the set and the historical trappings of the production, influence our judgement. We tend to expect that the more painstakingly accurate the set is, the more 'faithful' it is to the 'essence of Shakespeare'. Peter Greenaway's set for *Prospero's Books* (1991) immediately calls our attention to the film's seriousness through the re-creation of Renaissance paintings and texts which serve to enhance its cultural status. Audiences were disturbed by the 'non-Shakespearean' set of Derek Jarman's *Tempest* (1979) – even though the words were intact, critics refused to believe the film was 'true to Shakespeare', given the fact that the costumes (a mixture of punk and tattered lace) and set (a crumbling country house) were out of keeping with what we had come to expect of Shakespeare productions, as epitomised by the BBC Time/Life series. Televised in the late 1970s and early 1980s, the series was largely confined to doublet and hose. In Jarman's *Tempest*, the set – at least at the time of the production – 'de-cultured' the play text. However, McFarlane's final code, the 'cultural code', is problematic as it raises issues about the viewer's relationship to the film, the period in which it was produced and the period in which it is being watched. Clearly, our idea of 'culture' shifts; Jarman's film is now regarded, for example, as a 'cultured' text.

Similarly, connected to all of these codes is, of course, the time of the production; changes in technology clearly influence our perception of films – we are more likely to warm to a film which has just been released than to a film which is fifty years old, simply because it is technically more advanced. But the time of production also 'dates' the film, creating an ideological difference between it and the viewer; and in this respect, the analysis here differs from that of McFarlane's readings of novel adaptations. Although McFarlane's codes are a useful starting point, after a time, they blur into each other and/or change; visual codes often become cinematic codes, cultural codes shift. This book considers how films of Shakespeare focus on different issues (presented in the above codes and reflecting attitudes towards gender, sexuality, race and nationality) based on the time in which they were produced.

As I mentioned earlier, the subtext of popular films of Shakespeare is often the conversion narrative – that is, to inspire us with a love of 'Shakespeare', and thereby influence the way we view our world. This provides us with one reason why Shakespeare films are readily and effectively used in the classroom. In this sense, however, Shakespeare on screen can be a dangerous thing – and this book will explore how films can, almost imperceptibly, perpetuate a host of evils by sanctifying them with the name 'Shakespeare'.

Doing Violence to Shakespeare

John Madden's *Shakespeare in Love* (1998) features a young boy who appears throughout, usually torturing rats. When Shakespeare asks what his name is, he replies 'John Webster' – a dramatist renowned for his displays of violence. The film's success is, in part, due to its assumption of a dual audience: those familiar with Shakespeare and his contemporaries (and therefore able to identify the joke that this is Webster) and those who have little if no direct acquaintance with Shakespeare. For the latter audience, the message conveyed is that Shakespeare scorns the type of writing which young John advocates – 'plenty of blood, that's the only writing' – as well as the type of audience he typifies -according to John, the best thing in *Romeo and Juliet* is when Juliet stabs herself. The film itself moves from the violent to the romantic mode, beginning with the torture of Philip Henslowe, by the burning of his boots, and ending with Shakespeare, inspired by love, writing about love. In fact, John Webster – who snitches on Shakespeare's mistress, Viola, by revealing her disguise as a man – is the villain of the film. Viewing the film purely as a romantic comedy, one audience will go away convinced that Shakespeare was above the violent society of which he was a part. However, viewing the film with some familiarity with the Shakespearean canon, another audience may be somewhat disturbed in the portrayal of a romantic and non-violent Shakespeare.[22]

The representation of violence in Shakespeare on screen is noticeably diverse from one period to another and from television to film. A consideration of violence involves a recognition of all the codes discussed above: language (how much of the violent language is retained and the emphasis it is given), visual (how much do we see and how sensational it is), non-linguistic sounds (the tone of the score, shrieks, gasps, and so on), and finally, and most importantly, the cultural codes, involving the question as to whether or not the violence demeans or enhances Shakespeare's text. The exposure of violence in Shakespeare on screen is considered as a means of trivialising the text, as the case of a film which abridges the Shakespearean canon to a 'Theatre of Blood' testifies.

In a spoof horror film made in 1973, director Douglas Hickox has a Shakespearean actor, played by Vincent Price, take revenge on his theatre critics by engineering elaborate murders for them based on the plays in which they failed to recognise his talents. The film first plays back earlier Shakespeare films in a parodic fashion: Milo O'Shea, the friar in *Romeo and Juliet* (1968), 'replays' the role (pouring the potion for Juliet is visually recalled in the pouring of the whisky); Renee Asherson from *Henry V* (1944) (the courting of Asherson and

Olivier is visually recalled in the 'windows' sequence in the film), while a host of well-known Shakespearean actors ham up their own previous performances. It is a meeting of high and low cultures, but the incrementally horrific scenes which are re-enacted in what Edwina Lionheart (played by Diana Rigg) calls 'living theatre' bring to mind the violence so often swept under the carpet in discussions of Shakespeare. The film's title, *Theatre of Blood*, calls attention to an aspect of Shakespeare which is often forgotten, perhaps because to think of Shakespeare as 'bloody' sullies our pure, high culture conception of Shakespeare as something that is good for you and should not require a Parental Guidance certificate. *Theatre of Blood* daringly implies that Shakespeare is bad for you – in fact, as a result of reading and performing Shakespeare, Vincent Price's Edward Lionheart becomes a 'copy-cat killer'. His contact with Shakespeare has turned him into a violent serial killer.

The plays which are re-enacted include:

Julius Caesar   Michael Hordern plays a man who is hacked to death by a gang of tramps.

Troilus and Cressida   Robert Hardy plays a man who is killed and, like Hector in Shakespeare's play, his corpse is dragged by a horse in front of a crowd.

Cymbeline   Edward Lionhart chops off a critic's head, so a headless body can be placed in the bed with his wife.

The Merchant of Venice   Antonio's 'pound of flesh' *is* removed.

Richard III   At a wine-tasting, a connoisseur is drowned in a barrel of vintage wine.

Romeo and Juliet   The fencing match between Romeo and Tybalt is re-enacted.

Othello   Edward Lionhart, posing as a masseur, causes a jealous husband to jump to conclusions and suffocate his wife (played by Diana Dors).

Henry VI   Instead of burning at the stake, this version of Joan of Arc's execution is caused by overheating a hairdryer.

Titus Andronicus   Revenge is taken by forcing a critic to eat his favourite poodles – he is literally 'fed to death'.

King Lear The blinding of Gloucester is re-enacted – the critic, however, played by Ian Hendry, narrowly escapes Gloucester's fate with the arrival of the police at the last second.

Significantly, the *Lear* sequence which ends the film just narrowly misses the blinding of Gloucester and, in what is without question Shakespeare's most violent play, *Titus Andronicus*, dogs rather than people are baked in the pie. The critic's beloved poodles are stuffed into him in what is undoubtedly the most repulsive sequence in the film. What is interesting in this film is that it draws attention to the violence of Shakespeare on one hand, and ultimately, resists re-creating Shakespeare's violence altogether; aspects of Shakespeare are too extreme even for the Hammer school. This is not what we think of when we think of 'authentic' Shakespeare. Even the open-minded editors of the published Shakespeare National Film and Television Archive cannot disguise their repulsion to this film, noting that is often distasteful.[23] Hickox's film begins by showing bloody scenes from *Richard III* (1911), *Hamlet* (1913), *Othello* (1922) and *Der Kauf Man Von Vendig* (1923), suggesting first how – as Quentin Tarantino has demonstrated – violence lends itself to filmic representation and second, Shakespeare's dramas are full of violence. Why this mixture is not exploited can be explained by the fact that there appears to be a need to preserve the myth of a non-violent, family-viewing Shakespeare, that is, to protect Shakespeare's cultural status.

Arguably the most filmic of all Shakespeare's plays is *Titus Andronicus*; a play which resembles Quentin Tarantino's *Reservoir Dogs* (1992) or *Pulp Fiction* (1994) in its unnerving blend of violence and humour. However, to date, there is no major film version of the play – at the time of writing, *Titus*, directed by Julie Taymor, starring Anthony Hopkins and Jessica Lange, is in the production stages and expected to be released in 1999. It has taken considerable time for the play which was probably the most popular of Shakespeare's plays in his own lifetime (according to Ben Jonson in his Induction to *Bartholomew Fair*) to reach the screen. The play opens with a father killing his son in a fit of rage and follows with the revenge he takes for his daughter's rape and mutilation (her hands and tongue have been removed) and his sons' decapitations by baking two of the perpetrators into a pie and serving them to their guilty mother. The play ends, like *Hamlet*, in a bloodbath. The violence in the play is at least

partially responsible for its later unpopularity, as Jonathan Bate notes
in his edition of the play which attempts to rescue it from its lowly
place within the canon – critics, repulsed by the violence, have either
denied that it is by Shakespeare or relegated it to his *very* early juve-
nilia.[24] While today there is, on the whole, a lack of theatrical confi-
dence in the play (certainly another reason why it has taken so long to
make it to the big screen), this is probably the play which established
Shakespeare's reputation. If we accept its popularity (alongside
Thomas Kyd's Elizabethan revenge play, *The Spanish Tragedy*), then
we have to assume an audience accustomed to and delighting in
spectacles of violence. As Francis Barker has contended, Shakespeare's audience lived with a constant fear of death by hanging; the
calculation of those who were executed in the Elizabethan and
Jacobean period is staggering:

> estimated national totals for England and Wales including London
> and Middlesex are given by the addition of these aggregates. The
> resulting figures are as follows: 24,147.4 men and women hanged;
> 516.21 pressed to death, and 11,4440.52 dead in gaol; or, on average
> at least 371.5 were put to death by hanging, 7.94 were killed by the
> *peine forte et dure* and a further 176 probably died in gaol in each and
> every one of the 65 years of the reigns of Elizabeth and James.
>   . . . if a similar proportion of the present day population were put to
> death, at least 4,599.17 people on average would be executed as
> convicted felons each year, a further 98.29 would be pressed to death
> without plea, and 2,178.88 would die in gaol.[25]

It is perhaps impossible to know whether or not Shakespeare is
complicit with or critical of 'the will to punish' of the period. Violence,
in its many manifestations, was undeniably used as a means of
control. A taste for ritualistic acts of violence could have been
acquired from John Foxe's *Acts and Monuments* (1583), chained
alongside the Bible in every church, which describes (with engrav-
ings) all kinds of torture, including blindings. Certainly, the shocking
scene in which Titus's hand is cut off in an attempt to ransom his two
sons (III.i.187–92 – with the wonderful stage direction, '*Enter a
Messenger with two heads and a hand*') can be seen in the context of
sixteenth-century public punishments – such as when John Stubbs
lost his right hand for daring to question the Queen's judgement by

publishing *The Discoverie of a Gaping Gulf wereinto England is like to be swallowed by another French marriage* (1579). The description of the punishment is recorded, with relish, by William Camden, with in his *Annales*:

> Not long after upon a Stage set up in the market-place at *Westminster, Stubbes* and *Page* had their right hands cut off by the blow of a Butcher's knife, with a mallet struck through their wrists . . . I can remember that standing by John Stubbes, so soon as his right hand was off, put off his hat with his left, and cried aloud, *God Save the Queen*. The people round about him stood mute.[26]

Stubbs's fate is nothing compared to what befell others accused of treason; along with the actual execution an audience could expect 'sideshows' featuring dismembering and the ritualistic boiling of body parts.[27] Violence – both real and imaginary displays – were undoubtedly crowd-pleasers. George Whetstone, in an account of a crowd attending an execution in 1587, affirms that public executions rivalled popular theatre as a form of entertainment:

> I cannot number the thousands, but by computation, there were able men enough . . . the whole multitude, without any sign of lamentation, greedily beheld the spectacle from the first to the last.[28]

Ross's comment in *Macbeth*,

> Thou seest, the heavens, as troubled with man's act,
> Threatens his bloody stage. By th' clock 'tis day
> And yet dark night strangles the travelling lamp (II.iv.5–7)

although referring to the transformation of the world after the murder of Duncan, possibly also alludes to the theatre itself. Those sitting near 'the heavens' (the covering over the stage) would have to imagine that day was night (Shakespeare's plays were performed during daylight) and they would be aware, too, that the stage itself would be 'bloody' by the end of the performance. (It is worth noting that animal entrails were used in the theatre to ensure sufficient gore.) Just before Macbeth's death, Macduff teases him with the crowd-pleasing spectacle he will become:

> ... live to be the show and gaze o'th'time –
> We'll have thee as our rarer monsters are,
> Painted upon a pole, and underwrit,
> 'Here may you see the tyrant.' (V.x.24–6)

Macduff's threat implicitly places the drama in competition with real-life spectacles of violence, alluding to their popularity at the time of the play's production. While not being able to rival the horrific displays of real executions and tortures, undoubtedly the drama of the period attempted to imitate these spectacles in as convincing a manner as possible.

This chapter will consider the representation of violence in screen adaptations of *Macbeth* and *King Lear*. What becomes evident, when looking at Shakespeare on screen, is the ability of film to expose – perhaps to a degree which wounds our conception of Shakespeare – the violence of the language. When Peter Greenaway, in *Prospero's Books*, visualises the seemingly innocuous comments of Prospero that Ariel was imprisoned for twelve years –

> ... into a cloven pine; within which rift
> Imprisoned thou didst painfully remain
> A dozen years (I.ii.278–80)

– Ariel is encased in a tree, bloodlike sap dripping from his mouth discolouring his body – our first reaction may be to say that this is not in Shakespeare. But it is; and it is in the tradition of *Titus Andronicus* in which Shakespeare demonstrates an interest in visualising metaphor – especially those which are implicitly violent. For example, Titus, literally, gives his hand to Saturninus, the Emperor; Lavinia, literally, becomes speechless; Tamora's revenge, literally, becomes self-consuming. The violence implicit in the language is made strikingly manifest in the action of the play.[29]

Violence in *King Lear*

As a way of introducing the topic of Shakespeare and violence, this section will look at visualisations of what must be the most remembered act of violence in Shakespeare: the blinding of Gloucester.

Cornwall provides the unforgettable commentary:

> See't shalt thou never – Fellows, hold the chair –
> Upon these eyes of thine I'll set my foot . . .
> Lest it see more, prevent it. Out vile jelly!
> Where is thy lustre now? (III.vii.65–82)

Arguably, Cornwall's amazingly precise commentary on his horrific action has never been matched visually in the several film and televisual adaptations of *King Lear*. Yet, it would seem, the act lends itself to filmic representation as demonstrated in the surrealist film *Un chien andalou* (1929, directed by Luis Buñuel), which perhaps comes closest to revealing the repellent yet compulsively watchable representation of the mutilation of an eye. The unexpected and graphic bare blade descending on a woman's unprotected pupil made cinematic history. Surely this is the film equivalent to 'Out vile jelly!'; however, in spite of this filmic resource, none of the screen versions discussed below come close to visualising the repulsiveness conveyed by Shakespeare's words.

The four most available and most used versions of *King Lear* are considered here:

> *King Lear*   Directed by Peter Brook, 1971 with Cyril Cusack, Susan Engel, Tom Fleming, Patrick Magee, Paul Scofield (Lear), Irene Worth (Denmark/UK)
>
> *King Lear*   Directed by Jonathan Miller, 1982 with Michael Hordern (Lear), Michael Kitchen, Frank Michelmas (BBC)
>
> *King Lear*   Directed by Michael Eliott, 1983 with Colin Blakely, Anna Calder-Marshall, John Hurt, Jeremy Kemp, Robert Lindsay, Leo McKern, Laurence Olivier (Lear), Diana Rigg, Dorothy Tutin
>
> *King Lear*   Directed by Richard Eyre, 1997 with Ian Holm, Timothy West (BBC)[30]

Peter Brook adapted his stage version of the play for the screen and produced one of the most beautiful film versions of Shakespeare's drama. Filmed in 1971 in Denmark, the setting is early civilisation, the sets are bleak and inhospitable, emphasising the painful solitude of Lear and his associates. Gloucester's blinding, on first viewing, is an extraordinary piece of filming. In this version, Cornwall is clearly in charge of the torture; he brushes Regan aside so as to indicate that he is in control. Regan's 'Wherefore to Dover?' ((III.vii.53) is repeated by Cornwall to imply irritation with his wife for speaking when he should. Brook focuses on Cornwall, who prepares a spoon to scoop out Gloucester's eyes – when the moment comes, we see nothing; Brook plunges us into darkness and the point of view of Gloucester (played by Alan Webb). Reassured that Brook will shy away from showing us the gory act, we look ahead at the screen and, through reverse angle, the second scoop of the eye is shown – the violence takes the audience by surprise, and the impact is all the greater. In stark contrast to Cornwall's calm and calculated violence, Regan reacts to the rebellious servant by uncontrollably clubbing him to death. The lines of the servants trying to care for the mutilated Gloucester ('Ill fetch some flax and whites of eggs / To apply to his bleeding face. Now heaven help him'!)[31] are omitted; and we, like Gloucester, are left uncomforted by Brook's bleak vision.

Miller's BBC version with its mock Jacobean set offers us a more ordinary, explainable world and, accordingly, the violence is under-played. Gloucester (played by Norman Rodway) is immediately hurled into a high-backed chair which we see from behind; he effec-tively becomes a talking chair – whereupon it is difficult not to laugh. The emphasis is taken away from the disembodied Gloucester and on to the reaction of Regan, played by Penelope Wilton, who is delighted by Gloucester's torture, yet perversely, after the rebellious servant wounds Cornwall, she betrays a wifely reaction and rushes to comfort her dying husband. By focusing on Regan and by blending her cruelty with her love for her husband, Miller succeeds in defusing the violence of the episode.

The next year, *King Lear* was produced for Granada Television, set in a pre-Christian world and with Laurence Olivier, at seventy-five, in the title role. Yet in contrast with the bleak, snowswept landscape of Brook's film, the colours of the production are comfortable pastels and greens. Again, the emphasis is on the reaction of Regan (played by Diana Rigg), who smiles as Cornwall (Jeremy Kemp) puts out the eyes of Gloucester (Leo McKern). We do not see the mutilation – instead, we are struck by Regan's total indifference: unlike Miller's Regan, this wife does not rush to Cornwall when he is wounded. The suppression of the violence is best explained in the changing of the reportage of Cornwall's death: Albany is told that Cornwall was killed 'going to put out the eyes of Gloucester', rather than 'the other eye of Gloucester' (IV.ii.39).

In 1997 another version of *Lear* was produced for television, directed by Richard Eyre and starring Ian Holm. This a much more unsettling version than the previous television productions as this time it is Gloucester (Timothy West), rather than Cornwall or Regan, who steals the show. The setting is unidentifiable; in its minimalism and costumes (resembling those we identify with science-fiction films, such as *Star Trek*), the effect is one of alienation (in the sense that we feel alienated or distanced from the violence). The room itself, with a simple table and bare walls, looks like an interrogation room from a detective series, such as *Prime Suspect* (1990–); thus the familiar detective genre imposes itself on to our reading of the scene. Eyre produces a blatantly televisual version of the scene and shows us, unsurprisingly, the act of blinding in detail. The focus on Gloucester makes the scene much more disturbing than the previous television versions; yet, given the *mise en scène* and its associations, we expect the violence (unlike in Brook's, where it comes as a shock), and thus it is still anaesthetised.

The point of comparing these four screen versions of the scene is to demonstrate how television directors of Shakespeare shy away from the representation of violence. Brook alone gives us a shock, a shock which is perhaps more acceptable to Shakespeare on film rather than Shakespeare on television. By concentrating on Regan, the two 1980s versions suppress the violence, while in providing us with popular television associations (science fiction coupled with detective drama), the 1990s version prepares us for the violence which is ultimately 'unreal' or from another world. Although Shakespeare's plays are undoubtedly full of violence, screen adaptations, on the whole, it would seem, suggest otherwise.

Roman Polanski's *Macbeth*

When the media are full of arguments relating violence on film and television to actual criminality, especially among the young, it is not surprising that this aspect of Shakespeare has not been given full rein on screen, a point which the copy-cat murders in *Theatre of Blood* (perhaps unwittingly) make. The exception to this is, perhaps, Roman Polanski's *Macbeth* (1971), which continues to irritate audiences in its presentation of violence. Jack Jorgens, writing six years after the film's release, opens his chapter on Polanski's film with the remark: 'Roman Polanski has made so brutal and bloody a *Macbeth* that it is difficult to respond to on an aesthetic level, much less think about its relation to Shakespeare's play.'[32] In 1986 William P. Shaw, writing in *Literature/Film Quarterly*, considers Polanski's violence as 'distracting from the play's psychological conflicts', creating an 'exaggerated, darker, and less complex vision of humanity than we find in Shakespeare's plays.'[33] Both critics imply that twentieth-century audiences are more acclimatised to violence than they were in the time of Shakespeare. Jorgens explains Polanski's violent vision as a product of a violent life: Polanski was displaced by Nazis as a child, a Polish exile for most of his life and recently widowed as his pregnant wife, actress Sharon Tate, was brutally murdered by disciples of Charles Manson. The film was made after the Soviet invasion of Czechoslovakia and in the midst of anti-Vietnam activities in the United States. Jorgens concludes that in Polanski's *Macbeth*, blame is attached to society rather than individuals; and the violent society portrayed is clearly linked to that of the early 1970s. In order to account for the depiction of violence, Jorgens retreats into Polanski's biography, implying that violence is *added* to Shakespeare as a reflection on recent occurrences in the late 1960s and early 1970s, and in order to cash in on the vogue for violent films, such as Sam Peckinpah's *Straw Dogs* (1971), Stanley Kubrick's *A Clockwork Orange* (1971) and Polanski's own *Rosemary's Baby* (1968). Undoubtedly, Jorgens prefers to dwell on the 'prettier' aspects of the film (if indeed there are any), never for a moment considering that Shakespeare could have conceived such violent effects.

Polanski manipulates the text to suggest that Macbeth is not alone in his facility for violence and ambition. The figure of Ross, who after reassuring Lady Macduff, signals the murderers to enter the castle, changes sides after Macbeth fails to give him preferment; he then hypocritically delivers the news of the massacre to Macduff, and becomes, in this adaptation of *Macbeth*, a sort of Everyman. After Macbeth is killed, it is Ross who picks up the crown and offers it to Malcolm, thereby contaminating the future kingship.

The bear-baiting, the mutilated bodies and the actual dismemberings in the film are not supposed to be a part of the original text. Yet it was, evidently, 'a bloody stage' through and through, convincingly conveyed by this adaptation in its continuous red lighting. The violence in the film today seems crude – it is difficult not to laugh at the decapitation of Macbeth, as a sophisticated audience is incapable of seeing it as 'realistic' in any way. Interestingly, the seizure of Macduff's castle is the most horrific sequence of the film: the affection of the mother for her son as she bathes him is strikingly contrasted with their pathetic vulnerability in the invasion. The look on Lady Macduff's face in anticipation of what is to become of her and her family is the most frightening moment in the film. In fact, the women in the film can be seen to offer an alternative to the violent patriarchal world which they inhabit, a reading strikingly similar to that of Terry Eagleton published fifteen years after Polanski's film. Eagleton sees the witches as the unsung heroines of the play:

> [The witches] are poets, prophetesses and devotees of female cult, radical separatists who scorn male power and lay bare the hollow sound and fury at its heart. Their words and bodies mock rigorous boundaries and make sport of fixed positions, unhinging received meanings as they dance, dissolve and re-materialise.[34]

Significantly, Lady Macbeth in Polanski's film – played by Francesca Annis – is a far cry from the frightening figure of Lady Macbeth – played by Jeanette Nolan – in Orson Welles's film of 1948 where she, unmistakably, resembles the wicked Queen in Disney's *Snow White and the Seven Dwarfs* (1937). Welles's film makes the women the evil ones; Macbeth is doomed in his willingness to be led by a woman (that is, both his wife and the witches). The witches in Polanski's film, on the other hand, are not supernatural figures, but exiles from a patriarchal society; their matriarchal organisation provides a possible alternative social order. Lady Macbeth herself, who physically resembles the youngest witch, especially when we last see her, dishevelled and distracted, seems more a victim of patriarchy than an evil influence on it. Her sleepwalking naked links her to Lady Macduff's son (also naked, having just been bathed by his mother), reflecting their shared vulnerability and innocence. Compared to Jeanette Nolan's Lady Macbeth hurling herself to her death from a cliff, again in imitation of the evil witch/Queen's well-deserved death in *Snow White*, the final impression we have of Francesca Annis's Lady Macbeth is of a pathetic, distorted corpse which is all but trampled on by the male invaders.

Polanski seems to have broken a code of silence in his representation of violence and nudity in Shakespeare. However, the nudity is far from shocking. After the advance publicity indicating that the film, backed by *Playboy* editor, Hugh Hefner, would contain scenes of explicit nudity, a disappointed reviewer in *The Times*, reflecting on the coven of naked witches, laments these cronies to be 'little to the taste of *Playboy* readers'.[35] It could be argued that in Polanski's *Macbeth,* the women steal the show, just as in the two 1980s versions of *King Lear* where the presence of the women defuses the violence of the play. We do not see what happens to Lady Macduff; we do not see Gloucester if we are too busy concentrating on Regan.

The presence of women here, allegedly like their presence on the football terraces, keeps the violence in check. It is striking how screen versions (especially television adaptations) dilute the violence of Shakespeare's plays. When the language, visual and non-linguistic codes work together to stress the violence in the play text, then the cultural value of the product is, as in *Theatre of Blood,* drastically reduced.

2 Shakespeare, Film and Gender: Critical and Filmic Representations of *Hamlet*

To tell the history of Shakespeare on screen would take up many volumes, and rather than beginning with the first screen version of a Shakespeare play and concluding with the last, this chapter will concentrate on a relatively short period, in order to chart the rise in Shakespeare on screen not only in terms of sheer output of television and film adaptations, but also in terms of the increasing respectability of Shakespeare on screen within the academic establishment. Films of Shakespeare are, undoubtedly, influenced by critical fashions, and this obviously contributes to their acceptance within academic circles. This chapter will conclude by examining how different attitudes towards gender are reflected on screen through a survey of screen representations of Ophelia.

Shakespeare Films and Literary Criticism

In justifying the filming of *Henry V*, Laurence Olivier claimed that 'Shakespeare in a way wrote for films'[1] and, indeed, the film of *Henry V* succeeded in blending high and low culture, converting academics to cinema and the 'uneducated' to Shakespeare.[2] Books on Shakespeare on screen took some time to get going and accordingly to be recognised by academics. The following select list shows how few books on the subject were published in the 1960s and 1970s; whereas in the late 1980s, Shakespeare on screen became very much a developed field:

Robert Hamilton Ball, *Shakespeare on Silent Film: A Strange Eventful History*, London, George Allen & Unwin, **1968**

Roger Manvell, *Shakespeare and the Film*, London, J. M. Dent, **1971**

Charles W. Eckert (ed.), *Focus on Shakespearean Films*, Englewood Cliffs, NJ, Prentice Hall, **1972**

Jack J. Jorgens, *Shakespeare on Film*, London and Bloomington, Indiana University Press, **1977**

Anthony Davies, *Filming Shakespeare's Plays: The Adaptations of Laurence Olivier, Orson Welles, Peter Brook and Akira Kurosawa*, Cambridge, Cambridge University Press, **1988**

Bernice W. Kliman, *Hamlet: Film, Television and Audio Performance*, London, Associated University Presses, **1988**

John Collick, *Shakespeare, Cinema and Society*, Manchester, Manchester University Press, **1989**

Peter S. Donaldson, *Shakespearean Films/Shakespearean Directors*, London and Boston, Unwin Hyman, **1990**

Lorne M. Buchman, *Still in Movement: Shakespeare on Screen*, New York and Oxford, Oxford University Press, **1991**

It was in the 1970s that Shakespeare on screen began to gain 'academic' respectability due to the work of Manvell and Jorgens, who established a foundation for those critics who came after. Manvell's text establishes and examines the background to the principal films which have been adapted from Shakespeare's plays, while Jorgens takes a much more detailed look at sixteen films in the period 1935–70. In the late 1980s and early 1990s a huge increase in the field can be detected. That Shakespeare on screen became recognised by the literary establishment is reflected in *Shakespeare Survey* (1987); this specialised journal, produced by the Shakespeare Institute, devoted an entire issue to Shakespeare on screen and in 1994, its editor, Stanley Wells, co-edited a collection of these essays with Anthony Davies, *Shakespeare and the Moving Image: The Plays on Film and Television*. This collection firmly places Shakespeare on screen within the literary establishment. In 1994 I suggested that Shakepeare on screen be added as a category for review in *The Year's Work in English Studies*. It now takes its place within that annual alongside 'the comedies', 'the tragedies', 'the histories' and 'the late plays'. By 1996, it was virtually obligatory to include at least one chapter on Shakespeare on screen in major edited collections of essays on Shakespeare.[3] In 1997, *The Shakespeare Yearbook* devoted an issue to *Hamlet* and film. In 1998, Macmillan issued a *New Casebooks: Shakespeare on Film* (edited by Robert Shaughnessy) and at the time of writing, a *Cambridge Companion to Shakespeare on Film* is in preparation. Not surprisingly, Lynda Boose and Richard Burt's collection, *Shakespeare the Movie: Popularizing the Plays on Film, TV, and Video* (1997), has been advertised in the Routledge catalogue as a 'best-seller'; success may be due to what they claim in their introduction to be 'the recent shift from literary studies to cultural studies'.[4] Whatever the reasons, it seems certain that Shakespeare on screen is here to stay.

Considering the number of Shakespeare films, this is hardly surprising. The first recorded Shakespearean film is Herbert Beerbohm Tree's *King John* in 1899; but the film is only a fragment of Shakespeare's play, lasting only a few minutes. In his survey of silent films of Shakespeare, Robert Hamilton Ball suggests that an original reason for filming Shakespeare was to uplift cinema, to move from low to high culture – and, in many ways, this worked, as Shakespeare on screen gradually attracted the attention of Shakespeare scholars. But of course there were commercial reasons for filming Shakespeare as well. The first synchronised sound adaptation, Sam Taylor's *The Taming of the Shrew*, was released thirty years after Tree's; and it gives rise to the debate as to whether or not a film should record or adapt Shakespeare's play text. This difference between film adaptation and 'filmed performance' can be demonstrated by looking at Derek Jarman's *Tempest* (1979) and the BBC *Tempest* (1980). As far as the latter goes, the consensus among critics in the 1990s is summed up in Olwen Terris's reading of the television productions: 'The BBC Television Shakespeare: Weary, Stale, Flat and Unprofitable.'[5] But in the late 1970s and early 1980s, Jarman (whose departure from 'authentic Shakespeare' was largely visual rather than verbal) was attacked for his disrespectful mutilation of Shakespeare.[6]

The 'Shakespeare speakies' were produced not only to elevate the status of cinema, but to establish or display an actor's credentials: think of Mickey Rooney as Puck in *A Midsummer Night's Dream* (1935), Marlon Brando in *Julius Caesar* (1953) or Mel Gibson in *Hamlet* (1990). Clearly, film versions of Shakespeare are also made for commercial reasons which will be explored in this volume; we can establish reasons why Zeffirelli chose *Romeo and Juliet* to film in 1968 and why Kenneth Branagh opted for *Much Ado About Nothing* in 1993. Perhaps one thing that producers and directors of Shakespeare on film and television did not originally count on was their permanence. These productions are subject to unanticipated repeated scrutiny by students and critics alike. The risks of getting it wrong are increased as the demand for Shakespeare on screen widens.

Films of *Hamlet*

Of all Shakespeare's plays, *Hamlet* has been the most frequently made into a film and its film history is so extensive that it is the subject of Bernice W. Kliman's book-length study, *Hamlet: Film, Television, and Audio Performance* (1988). It is impossible to contain an entire filmography here, but a select list of major ('straight') *Hamlet*s indicates that it is a play that seemingly refuses to go out of fashion.

> *Amleto*, Italy, 1917, directed by Eleuterio Rodolfi
>
> *Hamlet*, Germany, 1920, directed by Svend Gade and Heinz Schall
>
> *Hamlet*, GB, 1948, directed by and starring Laurence Olivier
>
> *Gamlet*, Soviet Union, 1964, directed by Grigori Kosintsev
>
> *Hamlet*, USA, 1964, directed by Bill Colleran, starring Richard Burton
>
> *Hamlet*, GB, 1969, directed by Tony Richardson, starring Nicol Williamson
>
> *Hamlet*, GB/USA, 1970, directed by Peter Wood, starring Richard Chamberlain (for NBC Television)
>
> *Hamlet*, 1980, GB, directed by Rodney Bennett, starring Derek Jacobi (BBC/Time/Life Television)
>
> *Hamlet*, 1990, USA, directed by Franco Zeffirelli, starring Mel Gibson
>
> *Hamlet*, 1990, USA, directed by Kevin Kline and Kirk Browning and starring Kevin Kline (shown on PBS)
>
> *Hamlet*, 1996, GB, directed by and starring Kenneth Branagh

Arguably, the 'nunnery scene', especially its opening soliloquy, is the most adapted (and parodied) scene in *Hamlet*. Naming a few of the more well-known versions of this scene indicates its comic potentiality as well as its continued adaptability: *To Be Or Not To Be*, directed by Ernst Lubitsch and starring Jack Benny in 1942 (a comedy-drama set during the German occupation of Warsaw during World War II); *The Magic Christian*, directed by Joseph McGraph, starring Peter Sellers (1969), with Laurence Harvey reciting the famous soliloquy while performing a striptease; *Everything You Always Wanted to Know About Sex, But Were Afraid to Ask*, directed by Woody Allen (1972), in which Allen plays a court jester who delivers the soliloquy, 'TB or not TB'; and *To Be or Not to Be*, directed by Alan Johnson (1983), in which Mel Brooks repeats the role played by Jack Benny. Importantly, each generation appropriates the text for its own political and social agenda – that is, it projects its own cultural concerns on to the screen, concerns which distinguish the film from the play text.

Concentrating on the three major film adaptations (Olivier's 1948, Zeffirelli's 1990, and Branagh's 1996 productions), I will consider the films' representation of gender in relation to critical perceptions of the periods in which they were produced. Taking Bernice Kliman's statement that 'some films have found their inspiration, and perhaps their legitimacy in scholarly research and criticism',[7] a stage further, I will examine the interplay between film adaptations and literary criticism. A film adaptation is, as John Collick has noted, a reading in its own right in which the film endeavours 'to understand and articulate the values and truths that are supposedly embodied in the poetry'.[8] The original text becomes of interest for generating a plurality of meanings – values and truths – which Catherine Belsey describes as 'not fixed or given, but . . . released in the process of reading' and therefore, 'criticism is concerned with the range of possible readings'.[9] What is often shockingly apparent in cinematic readings lurks dangerously beneath the surface in literary criticism. By comparing film adaptations to critical readings, students can learn to question what they all to often accept uncritically as authoritative. Unknowingly, students take on board racist, homophobic, elitist, or, in the case of *Hamlet*, mysogynistic 'values and truths' when swallowing and regurgitating a critic's 'adaptation' of the text. In the case of gender representation, as E. Deidre Pribram has noted, 'the relationship between spectator and text is not fixed, but rather mutually effecting'.[10] Thus a 'feminist' spectator/reader/critic alters textual meaning from one period to the next.

In the scene under scrutiny, Polonius has discovered Hamlet's attentions to Ophelia and sets her up with Hamlet so that Claudius and Polonius can eavesdrop on their conversation in order to ascertain whether or not Hamlet is truly mad. It is worth remembering the previous scene in which Hamlet greets the players (with especial attention to the Player King – 'He that plays the King shall be welcome') and decides to try to catch Claudius out – 'the play's the thing' wherein he will try to 'catch the conscience of the King'. The nunnery scene is followed by the play within the play which begins with Hamlet's advice to the actors. Notice the attention to staging in this scene in advance of Hamlet's entrance. The scene with Ophelia is, above all, one of the many plays within a play – significantly the scene is followed by Hamlet's advice to the actors, 'Speak the speech, I pray you, as I pronounced it to you – trippingly on the tongue', announcing the obsessive theatricality of the meeting with Ophelia.

The initial question a director must ask when staging this scene is: does Hamlet look behind the arras and is he, therefore, aware of his audience and therefore acting the part of madman? John Dover Wilson in *What Happens in Hamlet* (1935) initiated interest in the dilemma as to whether or not Hamlet sees his on-stage audience – a dilemma which intrigued critics of the 1940s and 1950s (who almost never fail to refer to the problem) and which doomed Ophelia to being regarded as a traitor by Hamlet. Undoubtedly, this scene, embodying the problem of who is looking at who, provides an ideal opportunity to disclose the ways in which literary criticism, like film, directs our gaze.

Olivier's Hamlet (1948)

Olivier's film of the play came after his great success with *Henry V* (1944) in which film and theatre were playfully merged; the earlier film begins with a reconstruction of the Globe Theatre, and gradually moves out from a painted film set to an impression of real space.[11] *Hamlet*, as Bernice Kliman observes, is in a similar tradition, seeming to work 'against the inherent naturalism of film';[12] so we are aware that this is a theatrical space as well as a film space. The tension between film set and theatrical space is best summarised in Olivier's famous prologue to the film, 'this is the tragedy of a man who could

not make up his mind.' But the tension conveyed by the space disori-
ents the audience, making them unsure as to what is real and what is
not. This is the critical tradition out of which Olivier's *Hamlet*
emerged, typified by A. C. Bradley's interpretation of Hamlet's character in 1904 where the Prince is seen to be suffering from ' an uncon-
scious weaving of pretexts for inaction'[13] and T. S. Eliot's famous
account of Hamlet's procrastination in 1919. Hamlet is searching for
an 'objective correlative' which Eliot defines as 'the complete
adequacy of the external to the emotion'.[14] There is an obvious
tension conveyed by Olivier's *mise en scène* in the uneasy mixture of
film and theatre space; the set, dominated by staircases and closed
spaces, evokes a sense of claustrophobia. It also impresses upon the
audience that this is a domestic tragedy; most of the action takes
place indoors, the interiors being cold and labyrinthine. The film set is
perhaps informed by Caroline Spurgeon's famous study of the
drama's imagery, published in 1935, in which she describes the
atmosphere of the play as due to the numerous images of sickness
and disease.[15] The disease or unease of the play is reflected in the film
by the complexity of the set – the monochromatic film is both theatrical and filmic – which simultaneously closes in on the individual
while tantalising us with glimpses of spaces beyond itself, conveyed
by medieval paintings and views from the castle. In fact, the prison-
like castle is evocative of Expressionist cinema's 'interior-scapes',
such as Robert Wiene's *The Cabinet of Dr Caligari* (1920). It is hard to
miss the Freudian interpretation which dominates Olivier's film,
carried over from his and Tyrone Guthrie's 1937 Old Vic production.
This is a film with a woman-centred domination, as Ernest Jones (who
Olivier had consulted in the 1930s)[16] also suggests:

> The intensity of Hamlet's repulsion against woman in general, and
> Ophelia in particular, is a measure of the powerful 'repression' to
> which his sexual feelings are being subjected. The outlet for those
> feelings in the direction of his mother has always been firmly
> dammed, and now that the narrower channel in Ophelia's direction
> has also been closed the increase in the original direction consequent
> on the awakening of early memories tasks all his energy to maintain
> the 'repression'.[17]

Olivier was forty when he played Hamlet, and Eileen Herlie was twenty-seven when she played Gertrude; although she looks older, her attraction to her son is immediately apparent in the passionate kiss she gives him when we first see her. Jean Simmons is, at sixteen (or in some sources, eighteen), more like Hamlet's daughter than his future wife: a pitiable rather than admirable Ophelia, visually far too young to be taken seriously. This Ophelia is incapable of the rational 'O what a noble mind' speech and, accordingly, Olivier eliminates her one moment of glory. Ophelia's speech, when commented on by critics in the first half of the century, is only of interest insofar as it sheds light on Hamlet's character. This Ophelia seems too young to match Hamlet's powerful presence, and as such is blameless.

If we are to blame her at all, it is for being a woman (and therefore stupid); Olivier's reading is in accordance with that of his contemporaries' phallocentric views of the play. Jones sees Hamlet as understandably enraged by Ophelia's complicity with father and king, complaining of 'the hypocritical prudishness with which Ophelia follows her father and brother',[18] while Dover Wilson blames Ophelia for 'narrowness of vision and over-readiness to comply with her father's commands',[19] and the catalogue of her faults suggests that Hamlet has no option but to blame her: 'she had refused to see him and had returned his letters; she could not even speak a word of comfort when in deep trouble he forced his way into her room with mute pitiable appeal'.[20] Implicit in these remarks is the rhetorical question: what do you expect a guy to do? It is surprising today how both critics fail to recognise the power fathers held over their daughters at the time of the play's production. Ophelia is read as a 'real' woman, belonging to the first half of the twentieth century rather than as an Elizabethan construction. In the tradition of Wilson and Jones, Olivier intimates that she is both a liar and selfish in the change from 'O help *him* sweet heaven' to 'O help *me*' (my emphasis). Ophelia's duplicity is further suggested by the fact that Jean Simmons's Ophelia bears an unnerving resemblance to the boy actor, especially when Hamlet puts on his/her blonde wig (with the same hairstyle as Ophelia); this shorthand gesture succinctly brings the love and theatre interests together in the minds of the film audience. Olivier looks momentarily astonished at the transformation of the boy actor into Ophelia by the mere addition of a wig. But Jean Simmons's Ophelia can't even 'act' her part, as Olivier makes clear. This is a Hamlet who comprehends the situation he is in; he overhears

Polonius talking to Gertrude and Claudius, he immediately spots his guilty spectators behind the arras and continues to address the spectators in a loud voice and Ophelia in a softer tone.

That it is Hamlet rather than Polonius's death that causes Ophelia's madness is intimated by the film; a crane shot pulls back from her distraught figure on the stairs and she becomes increasingly insignificant – the tiny Ophelia is juxtaposed with the close-up of the back of Hamlet's head (which fills the screen) in the subsequent sequence reflecting their relative importance. Ophelia's dishevelled appearance, wretched and abandoned at the bottom of the staircase, is evocative of a rape victim and, as such, she becomes no longer of any use to the males present.[21] The movement away from Ophelia at the bottom of the stairs is accompanied by Claudius speaking the line aimed at Hamlet, but now applicable to Ophelia, clearly on the verge of insanity herself: 'madness in great ones must not unwatched go'.[22] According to Jean Simmons, it was Olivier's intention for Ophelia to plant the idea of Ophelia's future madness in this scene – her madness is initiated, at the very least, by the neglected love plight.[23] The love plot is magnified by Olivier, who shows Hamlet's remorse for his overly harsh treatment of Ophelia as reflected in the transposition of the 'To be or not to be' speech; it comes at the end rather than the beginning of the scene, suggesting that it is a result of his confrontation with Ophelia that he has come to contemplate suicide.

It is Ophelia's love (rather than Gertrude's) which ultimately holds sway as in the final scene, the Freudian overtones are abandoned for a return to post-war family values. The Queen, acting on Hamlet's advice, deeply suspicious of Claudius, knowingly drinks the poison in an act of supreme sacrifice. As Anthony Dawson has noted, the goblet (the one which Claudius was first seen drinking from in the film), moves from an image of corruption to one of redemption (with communion overtones).[24] St Veronica-like, Gertrude says farewell to Hamlet with the words 'let me wipe thy face'. For a post-war audience, familiar with sons sacrificing themselves in the war, this would perhaps touch a chord – a mother, here lovingly watching her swashbuckling son, takes the poison in the hope that the act will save him and he will survive her. The family has been restored, almost to the status of the Holy Family. Cunningly, Olivier ultimately places the women in the play in relation to Hamlet: Ophelia is Hamlet's beloved, Gertrude, Hamlet's mother. They are defined in relation to the dominant man in their lives.

The Hamlets *of Kosintsev (1964), Richardson (1969) and Bennett (1980)*

What is also noteworthy about the Olivier version of *Hamlet* is the absence of Fortinbras, Rosencrantz and Guildenstern; the political elements eliminated from Olivier's film are precisely those that the Russian director Kosintsev found so interesting.

Maynard Mack's observation in 1952 of the time being out of joint throughout *Hamlet* can be traced in film versions which follow:

> The whole time is out of joint, he feels, and in his young man's egocentricity he will set it right. Hence he misjudges Ophelia, seeing in her only a breeder of sinners. Hence he misjudges himself, seeing himself a vermin crawling between earth and heaven. Hence he takes it upon himself to be his mother's conscience.[25]

In Kosintsev's film, the time is genuinely out of joint as the director constructs a political reading, inviting us to make comparisons between Claudius's and Stalin's dictatorships. The castle is literally rendered as a prison; once Hamlet enters, he is doomed to the death sentence. Ophelia, as Bernice Kliman observes, is not the repulser but the repulsee of this film.[26] Hamlet, played by Innokenti Smukhtunovski, is too busy for women – his motivation is political rather than woman-centred and the sweeping aside of Ophelia is seen as evidence of Hamlet's self-denial rather than his misogyny. The overtly political and topical aspect of this film can be likened to the criticism of Jan Kott, Kosintsev's contemporary, who writes about *Hamlet* in the context of the experience of totalitarian Poland. He describes a production of the play in 1964 which opens up new political readings:

> The *Hamlet* produced in Cracow a few weeks after the Twentieth Congress of the Soviet Communist Party lasted exactly three hours. It was light and clear, tense and sharp, modern and consistent, limited to one issue only. It was a political drama *par excellence*. Something is rotten in the state of 'Denmark' – was the first chord of *Hamlet's* new meaning . . . Ophelia, too, has been drawn into the big game. They listen in to her conversations, ask questions, read her letters. It is true that she gives them up herself. She is at the same time part of the Mechanism and its victim. Politics hangs here over every feeling, and there is no getting away from it. All the characters are poisoned by it.

The only subject of their conversation is politics. It is a kind of madness.

Hamlet loves Ophelia. But he knows he is being watched; moreover – he has more important matters to attend to. Love is gradually fading away. There is no room for it in this world. Hamlet's dramatic cry; 'Get thee to a nunnery!' is addressed not to Ophelia alone, but also to those who are overhearing the two lovers. It is to confirm their impression of his alleged madness. But for Hamlet and for Ophelia it means that in the world where murder holds sway there is no room for love.[27]

(It is worth mentioning that this reading of the 1964 production of *Hamlet* follows closely Kott's later interpretation of Kosintsev's *Hamlet* in 1979.)[28] Kott's mission is to use Shakespeare in order to reflect contemporary concerns; whereas Dover Wilson's and Jones's attempts to be apolitical and transhistorical were doomed to failure. The 'objective' readings of the 1960s and 1970s fall into a similar trap.

Tony Richardson's production in 1969 is largely a filmed play, portraying an exceptionally epicurean court. The casting of Marianne Faithfull as Ophelia raises the question of her innocence – her pop-star status and relationship with rock star Mick Jagger could not fail to influence viewers. In the nunnery scene, she is made to recline on a hammock and the camera teases us with a close-up of her décol-letage. Visually, Richardson signals to us that she is a closet whore: her father's containment of her is a necessary one. She has what Milton calls an 'excremental innocence', an untried innocence which is, in reality, ignorance. This is an Ophelia who can only be innocent in madness, when she sheds the hypocrisy of innocence and reveals the sexual awareness which she has concealed for so long. Unlike Jean Simmons's Ophelia, Marianne Faithfull's is excellent at pretence; she convincingly pretends to be asleep and Hamlet falls into her hammock as into a spider's web.

This view of Ophelia is implicitly offered by John Bayley in 1981:

> Conditioned to goodness and docility, [Ophelia] is the exact foil to Hamlet's wildness, which means his native – though also indulged and princely – immediacy of behaviour. There is no guile in Ophelia . . . But there is a continuity, so justly imagined as to be taken for granted, between the girl who endures with suffering but stoical decorum the tasteless gibes of the man on the edge and climax of his

own private nightmare – the man whom she thought was paying his attentions to her – and the girl who reveals in her breakdown just how naturally familiar she is with the world of sexual innuendo and speculation . . . But schooled in proper behaviour as she is, and without much individuality of her own, Ophelia can still suffer as much as any girl, and she does suffer horribly from the cruelty of Hamlet, who understandably if mistakenly associates her behaviour with cunning and concealment.[29]

This hint of hypocrisy here is typical of Ophelia representations: she is either innocent in the sense of ignorance, or she coyly pretends innocence. Bayley sides with the view of Polonius and Hamlet, assuming women to be both inferior and corrupt. Critics, like directors (perhaps, like Hamlet himself), find her most perfect in death, where she is sexually passive and speechless. This is Ophelia's finest hour, where we, as spectators, like Hamlet and Laertes, can lavish attention on her passive body, untroubled by what she has to say about it.[30] Rodney Bennett's BBC version of the play, televised in 1980 and starring Derek Jacobi as Hamlet, coincides with Bayley's reading, which focuses on Hamlet's isolation. Both Bayley's and Bennett's readings are markedly apolitical (for instance, Claire Bloom's Gertrude and Patrick Stewart's Claudius are essentially well-intentioned and only, to quote from *Measure for Measure*, 'a little bad' (V.i.437); and both readings deemphasise the women's parts. In casting as Ophelia Lalla Ward, well-known to television viewers as the assistant to Dr Who (played by Tom Baker from 1974 to 1981), Bennett ensures that she will not be taken seriously. Jacobi speaks to her and looks at her throughout with a degree of sarcasm which the viewer, implicitly, shares.

Undoubtedly, *Hamlet* film-makers between 1948 and 1980 confirm the theory that in cinema the female is 'not a subject in her own right but the object by which the patriarchal subject can define himself'.[31] In considering representations of Ophelia, it is clear that it is not just Shakespeare who deprives her of a voice and an identity – it is both film-maker and literary critic alike.

Franco Zeffirelli's Hamlet (1990)

These male-centred (or Hamlet-centred) readings of the play are increasingly challenged in the 1980s, possibly inspired by Lisa Jardine's *Still Harping on Daughters* (1983): Jardine is among the first to articulate Ophelia's dilemma:

> Ophelia is honest (chaste) or a bawd (a whore) depending on how
> Hamlet now chooses to describe his own behavior towards her. If he
> loved her, declared that love to her, and she accepted his gifts and
> embraces, then she is chaste. If he never loved her, but attempted to
> seduce her only, then *she* is lewd and lascivious, because *Hamlet*
> trifled with her. Either way she should 'get [her] to a nunnery' –
> 'nunnery', as all modern editions of the play hasten to tell the reader,
> meant both a convent and a brothel in Elizabethan colloquial expres-
> sion.[32]

Conversely, rather than condemn Shakespeare as a spokesman for the
dominant culture, Juliet Dusinberre argues that 'the drama from 1590
to 1625 is feminist in sympathy' and that Shakespeare is questioning
the stereotypes his society imposed on women.[33] More recently
Elaine Showalter moves away from feminist critiques of Shakespeare's patriarchal discourse, where Ophelia can only satisfy father,
brother and lover in death (that is, once she becomes truly 'nothing'),
and suggests that Ophelia has 'a story of her own':

> To liberate Ophelia from the text, or to make her its tragic center, is to
> reappropriate her for our own ends; to dissolve her into a female
> symbolism of absence is to endorse our own marginality; to make her
> Hamlet's anima is to reduce her to a metaphor of male experience. I
> would like to propose instead that Ophelia *does* have a story of her
> own that feminist criticism can tell . . . it is . . . the *history* of her repre-
> sentation.[34]

Showalter combines feminist and cultural criticism, showing how our
perception of Ophelia is shaped by popular culture – her evaluation of
the play depends not on a reconstruction of the original conditions of
production but on an analysis of the play's reproductions.

Rather than look at Hamlet's tragedy in terms of a play dominated
by a single male consciousness (as Bayley does), criticism of the play,
such as that of the Marxist critic Terry Eagleton in 1986, starts to look
outside Hamlet:

> Hamlet is a radically transitional figure, strung out between a tradi-
> tional social order to which he is marginal, and a future epoch of

achieved bourgeois individualism which will surpass it. But because of this we can glimpse in him a negative critique of the forms of subjectivity typical of *both* these regimes.[35]

So Eagleton considers Hamlet's egocentricity as much an enemy to the state as Claudius's villainy – importantly, he stresses Hamlet's marginality to the society of which he is a part. Although this is a vast simplification of developments in *Hamlet* criticism, these readings of the play are not perceptible in earlier film versions. Zeffirelli's version of *Hamlet,* in its address to noticeably different spectatorial concerns, stands apart from the previous productions discussed here and clearly reflects the cross-influences of film and literary criticism. Zeffirelli's *Hamlet* starring Mel Gibson and Glenn Close can be regarded as a textual realisation in the same way as we regard the textual realisations of Showalter or Eagleton.

The first impression we have of this film is that we are unsure as to who the star is: Mel Gibson or Glenn Close. The latter's Gertrude dominates the film; she brings to the role shades of her earlier *femme fatale* roles from Adrian Lyne's *Fatal Attraction* (1987) and Stephen Frears's *Dangerous Liaisons* (1988). Indeed Close's role as the sexy home-wrecker from *Fatal Attraction,* whose extreme sexuality leads deservedly to her death, invariably influences readings of her Gertrude. Similarly, Gibson's Hamlet is influenced by his earlier action-man roles, and the film accordingly moves quickly; the scene changes are uniquely fast for the normally slow pace we expect from the play. Although the part of Fortinbras is eliminated, Hamlet's political ambitions are made clear from the outset. The funeral of Hamlet Senior opens the film, with the announcement by Claudius that young Hamlet is heir apparent. This Hamlet overhears/overlooks everything – and thus we do not doubt his clear-headedness throughout. The casting of Paul Scofield as the ghost visually brings to mind Scofield's role as Lear in Peter Brook's film – in fact, Zeffirelli's film is 'haunted' by images from Brook's *King Lear* of 1971 in its stark Bergmanesque exteriors. The casting of Ian Holm as Polonius gives the film further theatrical authenticity while Alan Bates as Claudius, like Glenn Close as Gertrude, brings a host of filmic associations to his part.

Ophelia, played by Helena Bonham-Carter, conveys the impression of a woman who thinks for herself. She manages to oppose the prescriptions of her father through her defiant looks and also interacts with Hamlet in the nunnery scene in a manner which challenges what the men expect of her. While Olivier's Hamlet and Ophelia were dressed in black and white, Zeffirelli dresses both figures in muted colours, visually signalling their equality. The nunnery scene is drastically cut (some of the lines are transposed to the Mousetrap sequence), in keeping with the rest of the film which, unlike its predecessors, shows little concern for 'fidelity' to Shakespeare. When Ophelia is abandoned by Hamlet, the camera, as in Olivier's film, moves away, making her incrementally small as she stoops to reclaim Hamlet's gifts, while the space around her becomes enlarged; but Hamlet seems diminished also, both are pawns, small figures against a massive system. As noted earlier, in Olivier's film, the smallness of Ophelia is juxtaposed in the following sequence by the hugeness of Hamlet's head, once again alluding to Hamlet's vast superiority over the helpless, insignificant Ophelia.

Zeffirelli creates a *Hamlet* which is watchable and entertaining. He animates the play by making Hamlet excessively mobile and by a succession of short sequences. In a sense, this is a cartoon version of *Hamlet* and bears comparison with the animated version of the play. When set before children, of all the plays in the animated series, it was *Hamlet* which I found generated the most enjoyment and discussion. This version depicts Hamlet as a child himself, unnaturally thrown into the dark world of adulthood. It is a story, after all, which is very near and dear to the hearts of children: who do you love best, your mother or father, and can it be possible to reject the advice of your elders? In 1994, Disney's *Lion King* was released, seemingly the only Disney film without a literary source. But of course, if we look closely, we see the most discussed of all literary texts lurking beneath the playful surface: *Hamlet* is present in the story of an Uncle's murder and usurpation of his brother the King and in the son"s gradual realisation of his position through the intervention of the supernatural. The hero's song, 'I Just Want to be King', is revised through the process of the film as he learns to accept the heavy responsibilities of life at the top of the food chain. Significantly, this version of *Hamlet* does not doom Ophelia to a nunnery, but it is the lioness and future wife of the hero who advises him to act and helps him achieve his goal.[36]

Kenneth Branagh's Hamlet (1996)

Kenneth Branagh's *Hamlet* cannot be accused of producing a 'politically correct' reading of the play, perhaps because (unlike *The Lion King*) it sticks so closely to the text. Filmed at Blenheim Palace and Shepperton Studios, it is set some time in the nineteenth century (with shades of *War and Peace*), and includes two interpolations of Hamlet and Ophelia (played by Kate Winslet) in bed. With this addition, her choice of her father (played by Richard Briers, who bears an uncanny resemblance to the then UK shadow cabinet minister, Robin Cook) over Hamlet seems disturbingly hypocritical (reminding us of Brabantio's lines in *Othello* I.iii.293, 'She has deceiv'd her father, and may thee'). As Alexander Walker, writing for the *Evening Standard*, put it: 'the movie makes it official: Ophelia was definitely no virgin'.[37]

In this light, Hamlet's feelings of betrayal are all the more understandable. Unlike Olivier's dark, claustrophobic sets (the only allusion to Olivier's film seems to be Branagh's similarly dyed blond hair), Branagh's set is brightly lit, described by Owen Gleiberman as producing the '"objective" glare of what could almost be a surgeon's operating theater'[38] (although this is not as apparent on video). This 'glare' is particularly hard on the women in the play – not just in making them look old before their time (the lighting sometimes makes Julie Christie's Gertrude look more like Hamlet's grandmother than mother), but in making them look guilty. This contrasts with Zeffirelli's positive images of women, especially Glenn Close's Gertrude (who, incidentally, visited Branagh's set when filming *101 Dalmatians* next door at Shepperton Studios).

While Hamlet is genuinely hurt with Ophelia's answer to the question, 'Where's your father?', his gaze throughout the scene is directed more at Claudius (than at Ophelia), who he comes to know is concealed behind one of the many mirrored doors. Unknowingly, Hamlet comes face to face with Claudius (played by Derek Jacobi, significantly a well-known Hamlet of the past)[39] during the 'To be or not to be' soliloquy. Branagh draws our attention to their visual similarities (especially in their closely cropped light hair and trimmed beards, also noted by Gérard Depardieu (Reynaldo) upon arriving on the set[40]); the simultaneous attraction and repulsion Hamlet feels for Claudius, he also feels for himself as he seems to wince at his (or is it Claudius's?) image in the mirror. The mirroring of Claudius and

Hamlet anticipates Hamlet's advice to the players (who look as if they have come from Dickens's *Nicholas Nickleby*) in the following scene: 'hold as 'twere the mirror up to nature, to show virtue her own feature, scorn her own image, and the very age and body of the time his form and pressure' (II.ii.21–3).[41] Thus his contemplation of his reflected image is, importantly, also a contemplation of Claudius (who similarly sees Hamlet through the double glass as an image of himself). Branagh chooses to focus on this pair, blurring the boundaries between observed and observer, actor and spectator, as we are not sure who is looking at who. Harold Jenkins, in his introduction to the Arden text (1982), identifies a pattern of analogies between Claudius and Hamlet; certainly in killing Polonius, Hamlet becomes a Claudius figure in Laertes's revenge on him. Jenkins observes that Hamlet, like Claudius, has '"hurt" his "brother" . . . and that the prince who reveres Hyperion and aspires to redeem his kingdom has also the satyr in him'.[42] Philip Armstrong has also concentrated on the mirroring devices in the play and comments that – even when they involve women – they are still masculine.[43] The focus on Claudius and Hamlet (at the cost of Ophelia) almost makes this a 'buddy movie' gone wrong. Nonetheless, it conforms to the popular 'buddy' formula (which includes films from *Butch Cassidy and the Sundance Kid*, 1969, to *Lethal Weapon*, 1987) where 'woman are simply ejected from the script'.[44]

Even though Ophelia is allowed the 'O what a noble mind' speech, the inclusion of her lines revealing Hamlet as the 'glass of fashion and the mould of form' (III.i.156) redirects the film audience's attention to Hamlet, Claudius and the mirrors. Finally, Ophelia and Polonius fade as the camera directs our gaze squarely at Jacobi, whose 'Madness in great ones' is spoken reflectively, and seems now to apply as much to himself as to Hamlet. Ophelia is hurt but ultimately unscathed by Hamlet's brutal accusations – there is a sense in Winslet's performance that she feels she deserves what she gets. In the Mousetrap scene, Hamlet looks askance at Ophelia during the Player Queen's (uncomfortably lengthy) speech, a speech which is an exemplification of female inconstancy. The camera shifts between Ophelia and the Player Queen, while Hamlet looks accusingly at Ophelia during the false protestations of the grotesquely painted (and false) Player Queen (Rosemary Harris):

A second time I kill my husband dead
When second husband kisses me in bed. (III.ii.175–6)

The Player Queen is the embodiment of Claudius's harlot, 'beautied with plast'ring art' (III.i.53) and a visualisation of Hamlet's rebuke to Ophelia: 'God have given you one face, and you make yourself another' (III.i.146–7). Significantly, the Player King (Charlton Heston), unlike his female counterpart, is not made to 'paint an inch thick' (V.i.89). Ophelia's visible nervousness during the performance clinches her guilt as Hamlet uses the play to catch her as well as the king. After the theatrical (and real?) display of female inconstancy, it is no wonder that Hamlet rails at his mother in the following scene in a tone which echoes Polonius's and Laertes's earlier warnings to Ophelia to preserve her chastity ; it seems that female sexuality is a dangerous thing.

Reading, like filming, is a form of 're-membering' the past, as Susan Bennett has outlined in *Performing Nostalgia: Shifting Shakespeare and the Contemporary Past* (1996).[45] Each film adaptation of *Hamlet*, like each reading, is a form of nostalgia, that is, a re-enactment of the past with an eye to its present-day consumer culture. What is disturbing about Branagh's 'nostalgia film' is its seeming desire to return to a time when women were expected to take the blame. Undoubtedly, the most striking thing about this *Hamlet* is its length, and as Adam Mars-Jones remarks, the film is 'redeemed by the one decision that seems perverse, even indefensible, the decision that is never made in cinema: trusting the author'.[46] A question open for debate is whether or not it is the full Shakespearean text or if it is Branagh's interpolations which doom Ophelia here. Alarmingly, in a post-feminist era, it is acceptable to blame Ophelia as – at least, in part – a traitor to the man she seems to have loved.

3 Shakespeare, Film and Sexuality: Politically Correct Sexuality in Film Adaptations of *Romeo and Juliet* and *Much Ado About Nothing*

In January 1994, 400 years after its original performance, *Romeo and Juliet* hit the headlines as one of the most controversial texts of the 1990s. A furore developed concerning its political correctness, thanks to a headmistress in a primary school in Hackney. Even today, the story (which probably has been long forgotten) makes bizarre reading. It teaches us that (1) Shakespeare makes national headlines; (2) his 'sacredness' is an issue which, for the most part, goes beyond argument; and (3) it is the *representation* (or reputation) of Shakespeare – rather than Shakespearean textual evidence – that is at stake.

It was discovered, some months after the event, that Jane Brown, headteacher at Kingsmead Primary School, refused a charitable offer for cheap seats at Covent Garden to see Prokofiev's *Romeo and Juliet* on the grounds that the ballet (and, by implication, the play) was blatantly heterosexual. The media went wild with the story, suggesting first that the poor children of Hackney had been brutally denied a once-in-a-lifetime chance to visit Covent Garden, and second, that this kind of political correctness was just short of criminal. The story was further complicated and blurred by Brown's admission that she was herself a lesbian and allegations that, prior to her appointment as headteacher, she was living with one of the school governors. The latter charge resulted in her suspension. As the charges against her escalated, the media were quick to reduce Brown to a cliché of a left-winger, complete with uniform. For *The Times*, Christa D'Souza reported:

> Making the comment was bad enough; almost as damning somehow was how absolutely Ms Brown looked the part. . . . Ms Brown defiantly faced the press in precisely what she always wears to work: a navy donkey jacket, red jeans and tan Dr Martens . . . To top off the look, Ms Brown was make-up-less with a bushy, naturally silver-streaked short back and sides and, best of all, a faint hint of a moustache. Martin Scorsese, who spent a fortune researching the costumes for his latest film, *The Age of Innocence*, would have been impressed. For Ms Brown's interpretation of the blatant non-heterosexual was so spot-on it could have been a send-up.[1]

A well-known strategy for dehumanising and thereby denunciating the enemy is to put them in a uniform; and this is precisely the stance adopted by a number of journalists in the case of Jane Brown. Even the more liberal reporters considered her remarks about *Romeo and Juliet* to be stupid and crass, commenting on her ideological idiocy, as Barry Hugill did in *The Observer:*

> Most of us laughed for obvious reasons. Ms Brown's comment was so silly to defy belief. She is, of course, quite right. Shakespeare had not much to say about homosexuality, but the only sensible response to that is 'so what?'.[2]

Although the Jane Brown story is dated, even parochial, it is worth revisiting for the media coverage alone, which makes manifest long-held assumptions regarding Shakespeare's 'blatant heterosexuality'. Even Eric Partridge in his glossary, *Shakespeare's Bawdy* (1947, 3rd edn, 1990), agrees with this view of Shakespeare. His introduction to his very influential and much-used glossary (proclaimed in the Foreword as 'well worthy of republication even – perhaps particularly – for the more liberated readership of the present time'),[3] instead of condemning Shakespeare, applauds him for having so little to do with homosexuality:

> Like most other heterosexual persons, I believe the charge against Shakespeare; that he was a homosexual; to be, in the legal sense,

'trivial' at worst, 'the case is not proven'; at best – and in strict accordance with the so-called evidence, as I see it – it is ludicrous. [4]

Partridge's 'so-called evidence' suggesting that Shakespeare was a homosexual and/or was interested in homosexuality ironically calls attention to the prominence of homosexuality within the Shakespearean canon and makes a nonsense of Barry Hugill's covertly homophobic statement that, of course, 'Shakespeare had not much to say about homosexuality.' Partridge, for example, admits to 'definite references to male homosexuality' in *Troilus and Cressida*, V.i.14–16 and *2 Henry IV*, I.i.14–17, and 'indefinite references' in the *Sonnets, Much Ado About Nothing*, II.i.33–4 and *2 Henry IV*, III.ii.326 although, bafflingly, makes no mention of confusion caused by cross-dressing.[5] Hugill suggests that Jane Brown's crime is in turning her back on her cultural heritage (the later charges against her merely serve to confirm her as a sinner). Her remark about *Romeo and Juliet* also implies that the play is dangerous insofar as it can be used to control, influence or regulate sexuality. The very fact that this story made the national news is evidence of Shakespeare's place within the British school curriculum and, perhaps more significantly, as a major part of our British cultural identity. John Major, to be sure, not an avid reader of Shakespeare, sums up the Conservative attitude to Shakespeare in a speech made to the Tory Women's Conference in June 1993: 'People say there is too much jargon in education – so let me give you some of my own: Knowledge. Discipline. Tables. Sums. Dates. Shakespeare.'[6] Taking his place at the end of this list, 'Shakespeare', the name, sums up tradition, culture and value, all that is 'right' and necessary for a wholesome British education.

The place of the Jane Brown story alongside other news items is commented on by David Selbourne, writing in the *Guardian* about the battle for ethical reform:

> Alleged satanic paedophilia in South Wales, phobic responses to Shakespeare, violence on television, and even the rag-doll vacancy of Michael Jackson's stare are seen, in however incoherent fashion, as common aspects of a mis-directed and mis-begotten world.[7]

The worry is that political correctness (which, incidentally, grew out of certain American Humanities departments' restructuring of the syllabus to include more female and black writers) has developed into a movement powerful enough to destroy our cultural values. These values are symbolised by Shakespeare; the fact that the much maligned Jane Brown was not taken to task on her suggestion that the playwright was homophobic reflects the fact that Jane Brown and her supporters and critics have little knowledge of Shakespeare themselves.[8] When talking about Shakespeare, they are considering a cultural icon, whose word has the same status as the Holy Writ. Writing in response to the Jane Brown controversy, Lisa Jardine, a feminist Shakespeare critic, defines Shakespeare's role as 'not simply our national poet, he is part of our national identity, . . . a shaper of those universal truths and basic moral values on which a small but civilised state depend'.[9]

Of all the plays, the story of *Romeo and Juliet*, undoubtedly, is the best known; and, unlike some of the other 'romantic' dramas, it seems to be the straightest: no gender bending, no women falling in love with other women, no mixing of races. Ostensibly, it presents an acceptable view of sexuality. The term 'sexuality' is used here to mean the social process that creates, expresses and directs desire and, to borrow from Valerie Traub's useful definition, sexuality refers to 'erotic desires and practices, including but not limited to the direction and scope of erotic preferences'.[10] The play's alleged 'safeness' – in terms of sexuality – is reflected in the fact that it has been featured on the English National Curriculum for fourteen-year-olds; and the tests, as have been discussed by Lisa Jardine and Alan Sinfield, enforce such straight interpretations of the play.[11] Its position, however, is becoming shaky; for those who actually engage with the play (unlike Tory ministers), it promotes under-age sex and marriage, street fights, gatecrashing, bad language, drug-taking and rebellion against parental authority; it is becoming evident in the classroom that the way the play is interpreted by students and more liberal teachers has little to do with or is in conflict with the way in which it is examined. The tests do not allow students to engage with issues which might damage the official iconic representation of Shakespeare.

The subject of Shakespeare's representation of sexuality is a vexed one in the media; as the Jane Brown case testifies, the nation does not like its cultural icon to be sullied. 'Sexuality' and 'Shakespeare' should not be mentioned in the same breath; reference to Shakespeare's homophobia, especially (although acknowledged as 'correct'),[12] is just short of a taboo.

Franco Zeffirelli's and Baz Luhrmann's *Romeo and Juliet*s

A film still used in the classroom, Franco Zeffirelli's *Romeo and Juliet* (based on his production at the Old Vic in London, 1960) premièred in London in 1968 with the Queen in attendance. Echoing the opening shot of Olivier's *Henry V*, it begins with Laurence Olivier's voice as prologue and ends with Olivier's voice replacing that of the Prince and speaking the epilogue; the use of Olivier as framing device serves to announce the film's place within a tradition of great Shakespearean cinematic productions. Initially, the newspapers' major criticism of the film was the casting of the youthful Romeo and Juliet, not because they were under age, but because they were too inexperienced to take on the parts.[13] Zeffirelli's film recreates fifteenth-century Italy and sacrifices the words of the play for visual spectacle – so the voice of Laurence Olivier is exchanged for the figures of Romeo and Juliet (played by sixteen-year-old Leonard Whiting and fifteen-year-old Olivia Hussey), who look the part even though their ability to speak the lines is often in question. Theatre is replaced by cinema, language by action. What is striking about the film is its use of colour and its careful orchestration of figures: so the vivid primary colours of the first half are transformed after the death of Mercutio to shades of grey, as comedy is replaced by tragedy, visually reflected in the darkening tones of the film. As Jack Jorgens has observed in his engaging and penetrating reading of the film, Zeffirelli uses the motif of the circle connecting the tragic and comic dimensions of the drama: the dance at Capulet's ball (a symbolic feud) gives way to the 'What is Youth' song in which a circle is formed around the performer; similarly, the duel is choreographed as a dance in which a circle is formed around the fighters.[14] Taking liberties with the text, Zeffirelli employs 'the gaze' within the film narrative, which includes both men and women,[15] to incriminate and/or account for the motivations of the *dramatis personae*. Lady Capulet looks disgustingly at her husband and knowingly at Tybalt. Her grief at Tybalt's death is thus more meaningful. (The gaze is used also in Zeffirelli's *Hamlet*, 1990, in which Hamlet's superior knowledge is visually explained by his constant observations of the others from concealed positions.) Mercutio's looks at Romeo are slow and deliberate, suggesting the latter has betrayed a long-standing relationship. There is a strong implication here of a special relationship between

Romeo and Mercutio now thwarted as a result of Romeo's new-found love.

Most noticeably, Zeffirelli accentuates the distance between old and young: Jack Jorgens reads the film as a product of youth culture in the ilk of the popular *The Graduate* (1967, directed by Mike Nichols) where the battle of the generations sides – predictably – with youth. Certainly the difference between young and old is emphasised by Zeffirelli in this 1960s production. Romeo is made less guilty through the film's deletion of his exploitation of the apothecary (V.ii) and his slaying of Paris, in which Romeo addresses Paris from a mature perspective, as a man to a boy ('Good gentle youth, tempt not a desp'rate man', V.iii.59);[16] while the old are made to look evil – even Friar Laurence, played by Milo O'Shea, goggles at Juliet while preparing his test tubes, betraying his lust or his selfish delight in the dangerous intrigue. Lord and Lady Capulet's attempts to control Juliet's sexuality reveal unembarrassed and undisguised child abuse. Capulet hurls the young girl around her room for her refusal to marry Paris. The older generation is seen to corrupt the innocent and wholesome sexuality of the young.

So, the lovers are seen as innocents in a corrupt world; their lovemaking is pure, symbolised by the whiteness of Juliet's room. Flashes of nudity (Leonard Whiting's bottom, Olivia Hussey's breasts) are only fleeting, suggesting rather than demonstrating sexual consummation. (Students have often said that in their adolescence, these well-known all-too-brief glimpses of nudity provided the incentive to watch the whole film.) As has been noted, Zeffirelli brings the two halves of the play together visually – and this reaches its climax in the death scene, where Juliet's bed is replaced with a tomb and sex is replaced or (as often is the case in Renaissance literature) explained by death.[17]

At this point, the film is about heterosexual love and the sexual climax of the play and the film is clearly the death scene. The eroticism of the scene is announced by the womblike vault surrounded with pillars. Romeo and Juliet's 'foreplay' (both seen individually embracing the bodies of their beloved, as if they were alive) acts as prelude to the ultimate consummation, which is, of course, death. Romeo, first of all, has to forcibly open the gates. Once in the tomb, he is located above Juliet, her face either off camera or in blurred focus. The excitement of the scene is generated, however, by Juliet's interaction with Romeo, reinforced by the quickening pace of the music signalling the coming of the watch. Juliet's entreaty to the phallic dagger to be quick – is answered, and she achieves the sought-after union with Romeo (which we are not allowed to see in the earlier consummation scene). Zeffirelli magnifies what Margarie Garber describes as Juliet's conversion of suicide 'into an allusively sexual act'.[18] Significantly, it is Juliet who holds the knife[19] and directs the final penetration which concludes with the two lovers nestled in each other's arms, smiling, as if asleep: a triumph of sexual transgression. They free themselves from the older generation's determination to control their bodies by dying in love. Juliet's final words are almost the final lines of the film:

> ... Then I'll be brief. O happy dagger.
> This is thy sheath! There rust, and let me die. (V.iii.168–9)

Zeffirelli omits the next 120 lines, which include Friar Laurence's explanation of the deaths and his part in it, and Capulet and Montague's verbal reconciliation. The Prince speaks the final five lines of the film narrative with a repetition of 'All are punished', pointing the blame at the older generation. The fact that he is the only one left speaking at the end reinforces the power achieved by the lovers; all other voices are eradicated in order for the lovers' power of speech to be joined with that of the Prince. His voice is replaced by Laurence Olivier's voice-over as the film concludes:

> A glooming peace this morning with it brings.
> The sun for sorrow will not show his head.
> [Go hence to have more talk of these sad things
> Some shall be pardoned, and some punished;]   *omitted*
> For never was a story of more woe
> Than this of Juliet and her Romeo.

The sexual climax of the film reinforces the message that youth is superior to age. Zeffirelli's lovers show little development; right to the end, they are unaware of the corrupt world about them. Thus the more mature vision of the play text is ignored in the film. Nor are we allowed the satisfaction of total reconciliation between the families. The Capulets and the Montagues reluctantly meet over the dead bodies of their children. Lady Montague is kept alive by Zeffirelli, reinforcing the unfairness of the young people's deaths (in this film, unlike the play text, only the young die). The dominant image of the circle is reflected in the structure of the film in which the death of the lovers results in no societal change – rather, the view is cyclical and therefore, cynical.

Watching this film today, it seems somewhat overly sentimental and a victim rather than a champion of youth culture. Zeffirelli's film, nonetheless, is daring in its representation of homoeroticism in Mercutio and Romeo, in the youthfulness of the lovers, and in its bitter view of the older generation: a far cry from the present-day popular view of Shakespeare.

Baz Luhrmann's 1996 film, *William Shakespeare's Romeo + Juliet*, shifts the focus from the eroticism of the central pair to the violent world which they inhabit. The updating is ingenious, if somewhat distracting (for instance, Mercutio's Queen Mab speech is now about his nightmarish addiction to drugs). Clearly the lovers are contrasted to the kitschy, Tarantino-style street scenes and wild parties, and we are presented with a clash of two types of film. The purity of Romeo and Juliet (played by popular actors Leonardo Di Caprio and Claire Danes) reflected in their simplicity of dress and their constant association with water (pure and transparent) is overshadowed by the more colourful world of violence which surrounds them. Like Zeffirelli's film, Luhrmann successfully reconstructs the play to appeal to a particular youth culture. This is achieved by modernising the set (late twentieth-century 'Verona Beach'), and using MTV camera angles and popular film genres, such as the western, car-chase drama and soap opera. The debt to Zeffirelli can be demonstrated in the feast/party scene where Luhrmann inserts a song (sung by Des'ree) in the same position as in that of its predecessor, allowing Romeo and Juliet to fall in love before their verbal exchange.

The film is certainly one of the most visually radical screen adaptations of Shakespeare. However, in spite of its technological and visual innovations, it can be seen as far more conservative than the 1960s version. Taking liberties with the text beyond those of Zeffirelli, Luhrmann cuts both Paris and the Friar from the final scene and allows the innocent Romeo to see Juliet alive the moment after he has drunk the fatal poison. The excision of the paternal friar from this scene makes Romeo and Juliet more mature and therefore more responsible for their fate. Upon awaking, Juliet retains only five of her original lines as Luhrmann makes her less transgressive and less powerful than Zeffirelli's Juliet. Significantly, Luhrmann rearranges the text in order for Romeo to be given the last word in this relationship – 'thus with a kiss I die' – befitting to patriarchal Hollywood. The scene – brightly lit by thousands of candles and neon crosses – lacks the intimacy of Zeffirelli's, yet Juliet awakes in what Adam Mars-Jones describes as 'positively post-coital languor'[20] and clings to Romeo's body, which convulses as if sexually engaged. Juliet's suicidal gunshot shocks us out of any thoughts of sexuality and places the film finally in the genre of police drama.

Kenneth Branagh's *Much Ado About Nothing*

The youthism and anti-establishmentism of the 1968 *Romeo and Juliet* is removed from the 1996 *William Shakespeare's Romeo + Juliet*, perhaps as it is becoming increasingly problematic for viewers today. For the most part, violence and drugs replace the representation of sexuality. If we want a so-called positive image of sexuality, we need to turn now to *Much Ado About Nothing,* or at least, Kenneth Branagh's version of Shakespeare's play, released in 1993, five months prior to the Jane Brown case. Perhaps the most controversial decision taken in this production was to mix Americans with British actors; but certainly this contributed to the box-office success. When the film was premièred in London, it was hailed with cries of 'bring on the Brits',[21] and the British reviews of the film could not resist referring to the fact that this indeed is a British production. Branagh himself capitalises on his reputation as an ambassador of British culture in an interview publicising the film: 'My future is absolutely tied up with making movies in *this* country' (my emphasis).[22] In an interview with Iain Johnstone, Branagh stresses that his approach resists being heavy-handed in order for the film to have a long life-span. This is reflected in the film's set – a villa in Chianti – and costumes – of a non-specific date and nationality – as noted by Alison Light writing for *Sight and Sound*:

> Branagh has certainly confirmed a move away from Shakespeare as the source of nationalist myth-making. Instead we have Shakespeare as a never-never land of the eternal present or mixed into a kind of

Euromulch. . . . *Much Ado* is only recognisably of its time by scrupu-
lously avoiding any direct topical relevance.[23]

On the contrary, however, the audience of the film applauded it as
purely British; and, on close inspection, it is as much a product of its
own generation's attitude towards sexuality as was Zeffirelli's film.
That it succeeded in reaching an audience is testified by the reviews
which are replete with words such as 'enchanting', 'sunny', 'fresh',
'unaffected' and 'life-affirming'. Branagh's self-appointed panegyrist,
Iain Johnstone, goes so far to say (on more than one occasion),
'Branagh seems to have a direct line of communication to the Bard.
He is unique in his ability to forget about any sort of sophistication or
elaborate interpretation. The play's the thing and let it sing.'[24]

The reasons for filming *Much Ado About Nothing* are explained by
Branagh in his introduction to the screenplay:

> Well, for me, because it speaks loudly and gloriously about love, one
> of humankind's permanent obsessions. The cruelty of it, the joy of it.
> The question of tolerance in love and the danger of judging others.
> The cost of the ambiguous maturity that people like Hero and
> Claudio enjoy. The loss of innocence; the power of lust; our obsession
> with sex and the flesh. The persistent presence of sheer, unmotivated
> evil in the world as provided by the Iago prototype Don John.[25]

The sentiment is echoed by Branagh's then wife and co-star, Emma
Thompson, who considers Beatrice and Benedick as an 'archetypi-
cally perfect blueprint for a relationship', 'total equals'.[26] The film is
made in keeping with popular expectations of the Bard; and it sells
itself to Hollywood in similar manner, as imagined by Iain Johnstone
in the following fashion:

> You can almost see him pitching the product to the legendary father
> of his main backer, Samuel Goldwyn. 'It's about this chick, Hero
> (Kate Beckinsale), who gets unfairly ditched at the altar by her fiancé,
> Claudio (Robert Sean Leonard), because his buddies say she's been
> screwing around. But it's a set-up, and the bad guy, Don John (Keanu
> Reaves) gets his come-uppance. At the same time, there's this wise-
> cracking dude, Benedick (Branagh), who is conned into thinking the
> even wiser-cracking Beatrice (Emma Thompson) fancies him.[27]

In short, it combines all the ingredients needed for success. First, it markets itself to the United States by using American actors and capitalising on a successful formula: Hollywood has conditioned our responses and expectations – if we see a man and woman feuding at the beginning of a film, we instantly know (due to the rules of romantic comedy) that they will be married at the end. Second, it sells itself to both the United States and Britain in presenting sexuality in a wholesome good-hearted fashion, stressing the need for maturity and traditional family values. The homoeroticism of the film, if it exists at all, is in the figure of the bad guy, Don John (Keanu Reeves); his evil nature is discovered in the darkened and steamy atmosphere of his dressing-room while he is being massaged by Conrade: stripped to the waist, with glistening torso and in tight leather trousers, he evokes a dazzling and sinister sex symbol.[28] The good guys – the heterosexuals – win in the end; and this is a representation of sexuality, validated by the immortal language of Shakespeare, which the British can be proud to export.

Unlike Zeffirelli's *Romeo and Juliet*, Branagh's film stresses maturity over youth and authoritarianism over rebellion. The origins of *Much Ado* can be traced to *Romeo and Juliet* as Branagh himself suggests; and as Ellen Edgerton explains, these allusions to the earlier tragedy are expanded in Branagh's film:

> There are further intimations of *Romeo and Juliet* in the film. Claudio observes Hero from below the loggia at the villa, echoing the balcony scene in the earlier play (as does Benedick with Beatrice), and [Juliet's 'I have no joy of this contract tonight./ It is too rash, too unadvised, too sudden/ Too like the lightning'] in Branagh's film becomes a flash of lightning onscreen the night before Hero's disastrous wedding. In introducing these, Branagh reminds us that Shakespeare himself was a master of allusion. Shakespeare's adaptation of *Much Ado* from his Italian sources, after all, might have been his response to audience demand for a *Romeo and Juliet* with a happy ending.[29]

Just as *Much Ado* can be examined as a refinement of the representation of hasty young love in *Romeo and Juliet,* so too, the films of these respective plays can be considered together, in particular, the juxtaposition of sex and death in the final stages of both films.

Claudio and Hero are younger than Beatrice and Benedick by about ten years, as Branagh explains, to allow for a previous relationship when the latter pair were at the tender age of Hero and Claudio (or even, Romeo and Juliet).[30] Beatrice's acknowledgement of her former love is stressed in Branagh's production. Facing the camera, she answers Don Pedro's charge that she has lost the heart of Benedick:

> Indeed, my lord, he lent it me a while, and I gave him use for it, a double heart for his single one. Marry, once before he won it of me with false dice. Therefore your grace may well say I have lost it. (II.i. 260–3)

Undoubtedly, this film concentrates on sexual maturity or ripeness, announced by the opening sequence in the hot summer sun where Leonato's entourage is characterised by skimpily dressed women, flesh exposed, eating grapes. In the first half of the film Beatrice is frequently seen with fruit in her hand, underlining her ripeness. The sexuality of the opening sequence is hard to miss: the men arrive on horseback, charging into the women's domain in deliberate imitation of *The Magnificent Seven* (1960; directed by John Sturges); this is followed with the parties rushing to the bathhouse, stripping off and washing, culminating in the men thrusting towards the women in a phallic 'V' formation. In the opening moments of the film we move from the words of the song 'Sigh no more' represented as a page of text, to Beatrice's voice speaking the words (significantly prefacing the film with her knowledge that 'men *are* deceivers ever'), to Leonato's picture of the landscape, to the place itself, and then to music and motion; and thus Branagh lures us away from the sterility of the words on the page to the fruitful or procreative world of the cinema.

The transformation of the painting of the landscape into a 'real' landscape also calls attention to the escapism of cinema – viewers brought up on Disney films will inevitably recall the device of a book opening into a film; and Branagh, perhaps accidentally, introduces *Much Ado* as a fairy tale and thus removed from the 'real world'.

As Branagh himself implied, Hero and Claudio function, in part, as a younger version of Beatrice and Benedick who are no longer susceptible to the pitfalls of a headstrong surrender to Eros. Theirs is a more mature sexuality, which is highlighted in the final scene which can be considered as an inversion of *Romeo and Juliet* (both play and film).

The final three scenes are rearranged: Benedick's meeting with

Beatrice is exchanged for the play text's penultimate scene with Don Pedro and Claudio before Hero's monument. With this rearrangement, it seems strange that Beatrice and Benedick have not heard about Hero's vindication, given the great procession to the tomb immediately preceding this scene. Nonetheless, the exchanging of scenes draws our attention away from the sullied love of Hero and Claudio; instead we are invited to focus on the older couple's preparation for the final wedding.

In the last scene of the play, Claudio's lines are cut, first to render his character less flippant, and second to restore the mood to one of romantic comedy. Instead of the darkened tomb (with, as in Zeffirelli's version of *Romeo and Juliet*, womblike associations) the action is outside in the bright sunlight; and death (and the fearful intimacy of consummation) is virtually forgotten. The careful excision of the bawdy and the melancholic reduces the tension of the scene and speeds up the revelation of Hero. Claudio does not mistake her for 'another Hero', as in the play text, but rather identifies her instantly and they become fully reconciled without a trace of recrimination on Hero's part. Quickly, all eyes are directed at Beatrice and Benedick.

This is a Beatrice who maintains her equality to Benedick. In the play text, Beatrice, like Kate in *The Taming of the Shrew*, is identified as cursed (II.i.16–17) and thus, like her predecessor, her wild heart needs 'taming', as Beatrice says herself:

> Stand I condemned for pride and scorn so much?
> Contempt, farewell; and maiden pride, adieu.
> No glory lives behind the back of such.
> And, Benedick, love on. I will requite thee,
> Taming my wild heart to thy loving hand. (III.i.108–12)

Beatrice agrees to marriage, in terms of total submission, accepting a lot of being tamed and 'handled' by her husband. The transformation is astonishing and we are right to ask, as Lucentio does in the final line of *The Taming of the Shrew*, ''Tis a wonder, by your leave, she will be tamed so.' Similarly, Edmund Spenser describes, notably in wonderment, the 'capture' of a wife:

> Till I in her hand her yet halfe trembling tooke,
> And with her owne goodwill hir fyrmley tyde.

> Strange thing me seemd to see a beast so wyld,
> So goodly wonne with her owne will beguyld.[31]

Scolding, witchcraft and whoring were the most common crimes of women in the sixteenth and seventeenth centuries and the censorship of the 'scold' (ducking-stools and bridles) puts the seemingly playful subversive speech of Beatrice into a dangerous light.[32] The scold or shrew was a stock comic character in earlier literatures – and when Benedick refers to Beatrice as Lady Disdain and Lady Tongue, he is possibly alluding to the early morality plays in which the characters represented individual vices and virtues. The reference to Lady Tongue is especially vicious, as the tongue is frequently invoked in its bawdy use as a female counterpart to the penis.[33] The tongued woman emasculates and overpowers her husband. As the title implies, the women are 'nothing' – 'no thing' is a common Shakespearean play on women's 'lack' of a penis. When Beatrice – against her original inclination – marries Benedick, she will have to speak the wedding vow, 'to serve, love, and obey'. In short, she will have to abandon verbal disruption and accept the 'natural order' of patriarchal hierarchy. For the play to be formally comic, Beatrice must marry Benedick as Hero must marry Claudio. But it *is* 'another Hero' who marries Claudio: a crestfallen, humiliated automaton who can only do what she is told. For all intents and purposes, Hero is dead. Assuredly too, it will be 'another Beatrice' who weds Benedick. Significantly, the final impression we have of Beatrice is of her being silenced:

> *Beatrice*: I would not deny you, but by this good day, I yield upon great persuasion, and partly to save your life, for I was told you were in a consumption.
> *Benedick*: [*kissing her*] Peace, I will stop your mouth. (V.iv.94–7)

Her mouth is stopped with a kiss – and so her linguistic independence is stopped by marriage.[34] To return to the film, Branagh ensures that this is a 1990s couple: he does not make Beatrice speechless when 'he stops her mouth with a kiss' but allows her to speak through her gestures. In the play text, there is a suggestion that the women have been 'killed', exploited and silenced through their acceptance of marriage. In Branagh's version, the men and women are, to quote Emma Thompson, 'total equals'.

In taking the threat of death out of *Much Ado About Nothing*, Branagh makes his film at once more palatable for an audience of the 1990s while defusing the eroticism of the play text. Zeffirelli's *Romeo and Juliet* highlights the intensity of young love by censuring the more mature vision offered by the play text. Branagh's *Much Ado About Nothing* does the opposite. The film begins with an overtly lusty atmosphere and ends on an exceedingly chaste note. The sexual energies have been subdued – Branagh and Thompson emerge as a restrained, older, established and quintessentially British couple, incapable of public or private displays of affection. Their love is validated by the older generation – most noticeably, Leonato and Antonio, played by Richard Briers and Brian Blessed, respectively – who symbolically join them in the dance ending the film. In the pre-Aids film *Romeo and Juliet*, the sexual energies are magnified; and this is achieved through damning the aged and milking the notion of death and orgasm for all it is worth. Branagh's *Much Ado About Nothing*, on the other hand, reinforces what has been identified as the popular view of Shakespeare's homophobia (as demonstrated through an analysis of the Jane Brown coverage); this is a film which distorts the text so as to be blatantly heterosexual and thoroughly British in its design.

It will be no surprise if *Much Ado* – Branagh's text- appears on the syllabus as a replacement for *Romeo and Juliet*. This is the blatantly heterosexual version of Shakespeare, in line with popular and, perhaps, wishful expectations of Shakespeare's representation of sexuality.

The Texts

By juxtaposing the film texts on to the play texts, the importance of the cuts becomes all the more clear. Just looking at the texts in this way illuminates what each director/writer deemed necessary to the overall thrust of their films. I have chosen to contrast the endings of Zeffirelli's *Romeo and Juliet* with Branagh's *Much Ado About Nothing* not simply because they are both set in sunny Italy but because they seem to me to be almost exact opposites, especially in their representations of sexuality. (Baz Luhrmann's William *Shakespeare's Romeo + Juliet* is also included here as a point of contrast, although there is very little to discuss as it retains only thirty-three lines, approximately thirteen per cent of the text.)

It is not just the plays, *Romeo and Juliet* and *Much Ado* themselves that are inversions of each other (*Romeo and Juliet*'s tragic ending is recalled and reversed in the 'resurrection' of Hero at the end of *Much Ado About Nothing*). The films present us with diametrically opposed views on sexuality. Notice how Zeffirelli's text eliminates lines which bring Romeo into disrepute and in which the older generation are credited. The ending of Zeffirelli's film seems to advocate unregulated sexuality based on a Romantic and 1960s belief in the purity and superior wisdom of youth. Romeo is elevated and purified by the omission of his killing of Paris and by keeping his mother alive (thereby preventing us from sympathising with the parents). Friar Laurence is made to look far more guilty; Zeffirelli makes him cowardly (notice the emphasis on and repetition of 'I dare no longer stay') and does not allow him his final explanation. Clearly, the young lovers emerge as triumphant over the older generation and Juliet achieves the ultimate power in her transgression, suggested by her voice giving way to that of the prince. The speed of the ending and the juxtaposition of the Prince's words with those of Juliet empower the lovers; effectively it is the youthful lovers who have the final say in Zeffirelli's version. Zeffirelli pays far less 'respect' for the ending of the play than does Branagh. Zeffirelli's text retains approximately twenty per cent of the original, whereas Branagh's retains about eighty per cent.

While Zeffirelli's film applauds the sexual transgression of youth, Branagh's film censors such unregulated and dangerous sexuality. Branagh's alterations blot out political incorrectness and anything which stands in the way of safe romantic comedy. For example, Claudio's 'Why then she's mine' (line 55 in the following extract) is eliminated as it assumes Claudio's view of husband as owner. In fact, all the lines, which portray Claudio in a dangerous light are cut (he retains just over half of his lines, while Benedick keeps about three-quarters of his). The many references to cuckoldry are eliminated, obviously for practical reasons as a film audience might find them obscure, not to mention unfunny, but also because these references make prominent the distrust and disrespect held by the men for the women. In the play Claudio retains his hostility and violence to the end. The emphasis in the film on Beatrice and Benedick and the excision of any mention of sexual infidelity – or sex at all – makes this a very 'safe' ending. By taking the threatening language out, Branagh makes a more chaste version, emphasising respectability, maturity and loyalty at the expense of the erotic energies present in the play text. In short, Branagh's ending evacuates the play of its ironies and its historical context, reconstructing Shakespeare's comedy into a Hollywood romantic comedy.

The texts that follow are based on Peter Alexander's edition of the Folio text (rpt. London and Glasgow: Collins, 1978) as it seems to me to have most in common with the various film versions. Words from the soundtracks of the films are in **bold** (Zeffirelli and Branagh) and underlined (Luhrmann).

Romeo and Juliet, *V.iii.74–309*

Romeo	In faith, I will. Let me peruse this face.
	Mercutio's kinsman, noble County Paris!
	What said my man, when my betossed soul
	Did not attend him as we rode? I think
	He told me Paris should have married Juliet.
	Said he not so, or did I dream it so?
	Or am I mad, hearing him talk of Juliet,
	To think it was so? O, give me thy hand,
	One writ with me in sour misfortune's book!

I'll bury thee in a triumphant grave.   10
A grave? O no! A lantern, slaught'red youth;
For here lies **Juliet,** and her beauty makes
This vault a feasting presence full of light.
Death, lie thou there, by a dead man interr'd.
How oft when men are at the point of death
Have they been merry! Which their keepers call
A lightning before death. O how may I
Call this a lightning? O <u>my love! my wife!</u>
<u>Death that hath suck'd the honey of thy breath,</u>
<u>Hath had no power yet upon thy beauty</u>.   20
<u>Thou art not conquer'd; beauty's ensign yet</u>
<u>Is crimson in thy lips and in thy cheeks,</u>
<u>And death's pale flag is not advanced there.</u>
Tybalt, liest thou there in thy bloody sheet?
O, what more favour can I do to thee

Than with that hand that cut thy youth in twain
To sunder his that was thine enemy?
Forgive me, cousin. Ah, <u>dear Juliet,</u>
<u>Why art thou yet so fair? Shall I believe</u>
<u>That unsubstantial Death is amorous,</u>   30
<u>And</u> that the lean abhorred monster <u>keeps</u>
<u>Thee here in dark to be his paramour?</u>
For fear of that I still will stay with thee,
And never from this palace of dim night
Depart again. Here, here, will I remain
With worms that are thy chambermaids. <u>O, here</u>
<u>Will I set up my everlasting rest,</u>
<u>And shake the yoke of inauspicious stars</u>
<u>From this world-wearied flesh. **Eyes, look your last.**</u>
Arms, take your last embrace! And, lips, O you   40
The doors of breath, seal with a righteous kiss
A dateless bargain to engrossing death!   PAUSE
                                    <u>JULIET</u> AWAKES
Come, bitter conduct, come, unsavoury guide.
Thou desperate pilot, now at once run on
The dashing rocks thy sea-sick weary bark.
Here's to my love! O true apothecary!
Thy drugs are quick. <u>**Thus with a kiss I die.**</u>
                        <u>TRANSFERRED TO l. 99</u>
                        Enter Friar Laurence

Friar Laurence	Saint Francis be my speed! How oft to-night
	Have my old feet stumbled at graves! **Who's there?**
Balthasar	Here's one, **a friend, and one that knows you well.** 50
Friar Laurence	Bliss be upon you! Tell me, good my friend,
	What torch is yond that vainly lends his light
	To grubs and eyeless skulls? As I discern,
	It burneth in the Capels' monument.
Balthasar	It doth so, holy sir; and there's my master,
	One that you love.
Friar Laurence	Who is it?
Balthasar	Romeo.
Friar Laurence	[*Balthasar*] **How long hath he been there?**
Balthasar	**Full half an hour.** 60
Friar Laurence	**Go with me to the vault.**

Balthasar	**I dare not, sir.**
	My master knows not but I am gone hence,
	And fearfully did menace me with death,
	If I did stay to look on his intents.
Friar Laurence	**Stay, then, I'll go alone; fear comes upon me;**
	O, much I fear some ill unthrifty thing.
Balthasar	As I did sleep under this yew tree here,
	I dreamt my master and another fought,
	And that my master slew him. 70
Friar Laurence	Romeo!
	Alack, alack, what blood is this which stains
	The stony entrance of this sepulchre?
	What mean these masterless and gory swords
	To lie discolour'd by this place of peace?
	Romeo! O, pale! Who else? What, Paris too?
	And steep'd in blood? **Ah, what an unkind hour**
	Is guilty of this lamentable chance!
	The lady stirs.
Juliet	**O comfortable friar. Where is my lord?** 80
	I do remember well where I should be,
	And there I am. Where is my <u>Romeo</u>?
Friar Laurence	**I hear some noise. Lady, come from that nest**
	Of death, contagion, and unnatural sleep;
	A greater power than we can contradict
	Hath thwarted our intents. Come come away
	[along];
	Thy husband in thy bosom there lies dead;
	And Paris too. Come, I'll dispose of thee
	Among a sisterhood of holy nuns.
	Stay not to question, for **the watch is coming.** 90
	Come go, good Juliet. I dare no longer stay.
	[repeated several times]
	[*Juliet* Where is my Romeo?]
Juliet	Go, get thee hence, for I will not away.
	What's here? A cup, clos'd in my true love's hand?
	Poison, I see, hath been his timeless end.
	O churl! <u>drunk all, and left no friendly drop</u>
	<u>To help me after? I will kiss thy lips;</u>
	<u>Haply some poison yet doth hang on them,</u>

	To make me die with a restorative.	
	Thy lips are warm.	<u>BACK TO l.47</u>
Watchman		
[within]	Lead, boy. Which way?	100
Juliet	**Yea, noise? [No] Then I'll be brief. O happy dagger!**	
	This is thy sheath; there rust, and let me die.	
	Enter Page and Watchmen	
Page	This is the place; there, where the torch doth burn.	
1 Watchman	The ground is bloody; search about the churchyard.	
	Go, some of you: whoe'er you find, attach.	
	Pitiful sight! here lies the County slain;	
	And Juliet bleeding, warm, and newly dead,	
	Who here hath lain this two days buried.	
	Go, tell the Prince; run to the Capulets;	
	Raise up the Montagues; some others search.	
	We see the ground whereon these woes do lie;	110
	But the true ground of all these piteous woes	
	We cannot without circumstance descry.	
	Enter Watchmen with Balthasar	
2 Watchman	Here's Romeo's man; we found him in the churchyard.	
1 Watchman	Hold him in safety till the Prince come hither.	
	Enter another Watchman with Friar Laurence	
3 Watchman	Here is a friar that trembles, sighs, and weeps;	
	We took this mattock and this spade from him,	
	As he was coming from the churchyard's side.	
1 Watchman	A great suspicion; stay the friar too.	
	Enter the Prince and Attendants	
Prince	What misadventure is so early up,	
	That calls our person from our morning rest?	120
	Enter Capulet and Lady Capulet and Servants	
Capulet	What should it be that is so shriek'd abroad?	
Lady Capulet	The people in the street cry 'Romeo',	
	Some 'Juliet', and some 'Paris'; and all run,	
	With open outcry, toward our monument.	
Prince	What fear is this which startles in our ears?	
1 Watchman	Sovereign, here lies the County Paris slain;	
	And Romeo dead; and Juliet, dead before,	
	Warm and new kill'd.	

Prince	Search, seek, and know how this foul murder comes.
1 Watchman	Here is a friar, and slaughter'd Romeo's man, 130
	With instruments upon them fit to open
	These dead men's tombs.
Capulet	O heavens! O wife, look how our daughter bleeds!
	This dagger hath mista'en for, lo, his house
	Is empty on the back of Montague,
	And it mis-sheathed in my daughter's bosom.
Lady Capulet	O me! this sight of death is as a bell
	That warns my old age to a sepulchre.
	Enter Montague and Servants
Prince	Come, Montague, for thou art early up
	To see thy son and heir more early down. 140
Montague	Alas, my liege, my wife is dead to-night;
	Grief of my son's exile hath stopp'd her breath.
	What further woe conspires against mine age?
Prince	Look, and thou shalt see.
Montague	O thou untaught! what manners is in this,
	To press before thy father to a grave?
Prince	Seal up the mouth of outrage for a while,
	Till we can clear these ambiguities,
	And know their spring, their head, their true descent;
	And then will I be general of your woes, 150
	And lead you even to death. Meantime forbear,
	And let mischance be slave to patience.
	Bring forth the parties of suspicion.
Friar Laurence	I am the greatest, able to do least,
	Yet most suspected, as the time and place
	Doth make against me, of this direful murder;
	And here I stand, both to impeach and purge
	Myself condemned and myself excus'd.
Prince	Then say at once what thou dost know in this.
Friar Laurence	I will be brief, for my short date of breath 160
	Is not so long as is a tedious tale.
	Romeo, there dead, was husband to that Juliet;
	And she, there dead, that Romeo's faithful wife.
	I married them; and their stol'n marriage-day
	Was Tybalt's doomsday, whose untimely death
	Banish'd the new-made bridegroom from this city;

For whom, and not for Tybalt, Juliet pin'd.
You, to remove that siege of grief from her,
Betroth'd, and would have married her perforce,
To County Paris. Then comes she to me,   170
And with wild looks bid me devise some mean
To rid her from this second marriage,
Or in my cell there would she kill herself.
Then gave I her, so tutor'd by my art,
A sleeping potion; which so took effect
As I intended, for it wrought on her
The form of death. Meantime I writ to Romeo
That he should hither come as this dire night
To help to take her from her borrowed grave,
Being the time the potion's force should cease.   180
But he which bore my letter, Friar John,
Was stay'd by accident, and yesternight
Return'd my letter back. Then all alone
At the prefixed hour of her waking
Came I to take her from her kindred's vault;
Meaning to keep her closely at my cell
Till I conveniently could send to Romeo.
But when I came, some minute ere the time
Of her awakening, here untimely lay
The noble Paris and true Romeo dead.   190
She wakes; and I entreated her come forth,
And bear this work of heaven with patience.
But then a noise did scare me from the tomb,
And she, too desperate, would not go with me,
But, as it seems, did violence on herself.
All this I know; and to the marriage
Her nurse is privy; and if ought in this
Miscarried by my fault, let my old life
Be sacrific'd, some hour before his time,
Unto the rigour of severest law.   200

Prince   We still have known thee for a holy man.
             Where's Romeo's man? What can he say to this?

Balthasar I brought my master news of Juliet's death;
             And then in post he came from Mantua
             To this same place, to this same monument.

	This letter he early bid me give his father;	
	And threaten'd me with death, going in the vault,	
	If I departed not and left him there.	
Prince	Give me the letter, I will look on it.	
	Where is the County's Page that rais'd the watch?	210
	Sirrah, what made your master in this place?	
Page	He came with flowers to strew his lady's grave;	
	And bid me stand aloof, and so I did.	
	Anon comes one with light to ope the tomb;	
	And by and by my master drew on him;	
	And then I ran away to call the watch.	
Prince	This letter doth make good the friar's words,	
	Their course of love, the tidings of her death;	
	And here he writes that he did buy a poison	
	Of a poor pothecary, and therewithal	220
	Came to this vault to die, and lie with Juliet.	
	Where be these enemies? Capulet, Montague,	
	See what a scourge is laid upon your hate,	
	That heaven finds means to kill your joys with love!	
	And I, for winking at your discords too,	
	Have lost a brace of kinsmen. All are punish'd.	
	['**All are punished**' repeated]	
Capulet	O brother Montague, give me thy hand.	
	This is my daughter's jointure, for no more	
	Can I demand.	
Montague:	But I can give thee more;	230
	For I will raise her statue in pure gold,	
	That whiles Verona by that name is known,	
	There shall no figure at such rate be set	
	As that of true and faithful Juliet.	
Capulet	As rich shall Romeo's by his lady's lie –	
	Poor sacrifices of our enmity!	
Prince /	**A glooming peace this morning with it brings;**	
Narrator/	**The sun for sorrow will not show his head.**	
Anchorwoman	Go hence, to have more talk of these sad things;	
	Some shall be pardon'd and some punished;	240
	For never was a story of more woe	
	Than this of Juliet and her Romeo.	

Much Ado About Nothing, *V.iv (Branagh's film soundtrack is shown in **bold**)*

Friar	**Did I not tell you she was innocent?**
Leonato	**So are the Prince and Claudio, who accus'd her**
	Upon the error that you heard debated.
	But Margaret was in some fault for this,
	Although against her will, as it appears
	In the true course of all the question.
Antonio	**Well, I am glad that all things sorts so well.**
Benedick	And so am I, being else by faith enforc'd
	To call young Claudio to a reckoning for it.
Leonato	**Well, daughter, and you gentlewomen all,** 10
	Withdraw into a chamber by yourselves;
	And when I send for you, come hither mask'd.
	The Prince and Claudio promis'd by this hour
	To visit me. You know your office, brother:
	You must be father to your brother's daughter,
	And give her to young Claudio.
Antonio	**Which I will do with confirm'd countenance.**
Benedick	**Friar, I must entreat your pains, I think.**
Friar	**To do what, signior?**
Benedick	**To bind me, or undo me – one of them.** 20
	Signior Leonato, truth it is, good signior,
	Your niece regards me with an eye of favour.
Leonato	That eye my daughter lent her. 'Tis most true.
Benedick	And I do with an eye of love requite her.
Leonato	**The sight whereof, I think, you had from me,**
	From Claudio, and the Prince. But what's your will?
Benedick	**Your answer, sir, is enigmatical.**
	But, for my will, my will is, your good will
	May stand with ours, this day to be conjoin'd
	In the state of honourable marriage; ['honourable'
	changed to **horrible**] 30
	In which, good friar, I shall desire your help.
Leonato	**My heart is with your liking.**
Friar	**And my help.**
	Here comes the Prince and Claudio.
Don Pedro	**Good morrow to this fair assembly.**

Leonato	Good morrow, Prince; good morrow, Claudio;
	We here attend you. Are you yet determin'd
	To-day to marry with my brother's daughter?
Claudio	I'll hold my mind were she an Ethiope. [Nods]
Leonato	Call her forth, brother; here's the friar ready.
Don Pedro	Good morrow, Benedick. Why, what's the matter 40
	That you have such a February face,
	So full of frost, of storm, and cloudiness?
Claudio	I think he thinks upon the savage bull.
	Tush, fear not, man; we'll tip thy horns with gold,
	And all Europa shall rejoice at thee,
	As once Europa did at lusty Jove,
	When he would play the noble beast in love.
Benedick	Bull Jove, sir, had an amiable low;
	And some such strange bull leap'd your father's cow,
	And got a calf in that same noble feat 50
	Much like to you, for you have just his bleat.
Claudio	For this I owe you: here comes other reck'nings.
	Which is the lady I must seize upon?
Antonio	This same is she, and I do give you her.
Claudio	Why, then she's mine. Sweet, let me see your face.
Leonato	No, that you shall not, till you take her hand,
	Before this friar, and swear to marry her.
Claudio	Give me your hand; before this holy friar
	I am your husband if you like of me.

*   *   *

(Branagh's text transposes the following lines)

BRANAGH'S TEXT

Hero:	And when I liv'd I was your other wife; 60	Don Pedro:	Hero that is dead!
	And when you lov'd you were my other husband.		
Claudio:	Another Hero!	Leonato:	She died, my lord, but whiles her slander liv'd.

Hero:	Nothing certainer.	Hero:	And when I

Hero: Nothing certainer.
            One Hero died defil'd, but I do live,
            And, surely as I live, I am a maid.

Hero: And when I
            liv'd I was your
            other wife;/
            And when you
            lov'd you were
            my other
            husband./
            One Hero died
            defil'd, but I do
            live,/
            And, surely as I
            live, I am a
            maid.

Don Pedro: The former Hero! **Hero that is dead!**
Leonato: **She died, my lord, but whiles her slander liv'd.**

*   *   *

Friar	All this amazement can I qualify,	
	When, after that the holy rites are ended,	
	I'll tell you largely of fair Hero's death.	
	Meantime let wonder seem familiar,	70
	And to the chapel let us presently.	
Benedick	**Soft and fair, friar. Which is Beatrice?**	
Beatrice	**I answer to that name. What is your will?**	
Benedick	**Do not you love me?**	
Beatrice	Why, no, no more than reason.	
Benedick	**Why, then your uncle, and the Prince, and Claudio,**	
	Have been deceived: they swore you did.	
Beatrice	**Do not you love me?**	
Benedick	[Troth] **no, no more than reason.**	
Beatrice	**Why, then my cousin, Margaret, and Ursula,**	
	Are much deceiv'd; for they did swear you did.	
Benedick	**They swore that you were almost sick for me.**	80
Beatrice	**They swore that you were well-nigh dead for me.**	
Benedick	**'Tis no such matter. Then you do not love me?**	
Beatrice	**No, truly, but in friendly recompense.**	
Leonato	**Come, cousin, I am sure you love the gentleman.**	

Claudio	And I'll be sworn upon't that he loves her;
	For here's a paper written in his hand,
	A halting sonnet of his own pure brain,
	Fashion'd to Beatrice.
Hero	And here's another,
	Writ in my cousin's hand, stol'n from her pocket,
	Containing her affection unto Benedick. 90
Benedick	A miracle! Here's our own hands against our hearts.
	Come, I will have thee; but, by this light, I take thee
	for pity.
Beatrice	I would not deny you; but by this good day, I yield
	upon great persuasion; and partly to save your life,
	for I was told you were in a consumption.
Benedick	Peace; I will stop your mouth.
Don Pedro	How dost thou, Benedick the married man?
Benedick	I'll tell thee what, Prince: a college of wit-crackers
	cannot flout me out of my humour. Dost thou think
	I care for a satire or an epigram? No. If a man will be
	beaten with brains, 'a shall wear nothing handsome
	about him. In brief, since I do purpose to marry, I will
	think nothing to any purpose that the world can say
	against it; and therefore never flout at me for what I
	have said against it; for man is a giddy thing, and
	this is my conclusion. For thy part, Claudio, I did
	think to have beaten thee; but in that thou art like
	to be my kinsman, live unbruis'd, and love my
	cousin. 104
Claudio	I had well hop'd thou wouldst have denied Beatrice,
	that I might have cudgell'd thee out of thy single life,
	to make thee a double dealer; which out of question
	thou wilt be, if my cousin do not look exceeding
	narrowly to thee.
Benedick	Come, come, we are friends. Let's have a dance ere
	we are married, that we may lighten our own hearts
	and our wives' heels.
Leonato	We'll have dancing afterward. 110
Benedick	First, of my word; therefore play, music. Prince,
	thou art sad; get thee a wife, get thee a wife. There
	is no staff more reverend than one tipp'd with horn.

Messenger	My lord, your brother John is ta'en in flight,
	And brought with armed men back to Messina.
Benedick	Think not on him till to-morrow. I'll devise thee brave
	punishments for him. Strike up, pipers.

4 Shakespeare, Film and Race: Screening *Othello* and *The Tempest*

Graham Bradshaw complains in *Misrepresentations: Shakespeare and the Materialists*[1] that the question of whether or not Shakespeare is racist or not has reduced texts like *Othello* and *The Tempest* to the level of evidence, placing critics in the roles of lawyers for the prosecution, labouring to 'prove' Shakespeare's guilt. Until recently, the notion that Shakespeare (like all gentlemen) preferred blondes was accepted without challenge or blame in both literary criticism and film and televisual productions – an assumption that reflects the critic's and director's (rather than Shakespeare's) unknowing racism. In spite of recent readings of the representation of race in Shakespeare, films of these plays, no matter how experimental in form, remain fundamentally conservative in their representation of race, conforming to what James Monaco argues is the Hollywood norm. Monaco asserts that 'racism pervades American film because it is a basic strain in American history. It is one of the ugly facts that the landmark *The Birth of a Nation* (1915) can be generally hailed as a classic despite its essential racism.'[2] In attempting to ignore race, so much the concern of recent Shakespeare criticism, recent films of *The Tempest* and *Othello*, even when seemingly striving for 'political correctness', fall into the Hollywood racial trap.

'Black'[3] people feature in a number of Shakespeare's works. The most notorious is probably Aaron, the moor in *Titus Andronicus,* whose excessively violent behaviour is identified as devilish 'acts of black night' (V.i.64). The Prince of Morocco, in *The Merchant of Venice,* briefly threatens Portia with miscegenation, inspiring her relief at his failure to wed her with the words 'Let all of his complexion choose me so' (II.vii.79). The poet of the *Sonnets* seemingly conforms to the commonly held view that a dark complexion reflects an evil nature. He says to his 'dark lady', 'For I have sworn thee fair, and thought thee bright, / Who art as black as hell, as dark as night' (147). Cleopatra's blackness is linked to her exotic sexual appetite as she says of herself, 'Think on me, / That am with Phoebus' amorous pinches black' (I.v.27–8). Blackness is regarded by white characters in the manner of Claudio in *Much Ado* who, repentant for his treatment of Hero, 'magnanimously' agrees to marry anyone – 'I'll hold my mind, were she an Ethiope' (V.iv.38), a line almost always cut from productions of the play. Why this line is so often deleted is worth exploring; and this chapter aims to consider the changing filmic representations of the two best known of Shakespeare's black characters – Othello and Caliban.

In this chapter, Othello and Caliban are taken together as – in many ways – they are similar representations of 'black' men. Both commit real or attempted miscegenation; Othello's 'wooing', however, 'succeeds' where Caliban's fails. In Shakespeare (on the whole, if taken literally), a white woman who agrees to a sexual alliance with a black man is morally tainted, as in *Titus Andronicus* where Tamora's sexual alliance with Aaron the moor confirms her wickedness. Aaron represents the extreme stereotype, referring to himself 'like a black dog' (V.i.122); so extreme is he in his wickedness that it is possible his representation is a parody of the stereotype of the evil and lascivious moor. In *Two Gentlemen of Verona*, Julia's disavowal of Proteus's remark,

> But pearls are fair; and the old saying is,
> "Black men are pearls in beauteous ladies' eyes".
> *Julia*: [*Aside*] 'Tis true, such pearls as put out ladies' eyes,
> For I had rather wink than look on them. (V.ii.11–14)

confirms her chastity – or lack of sexuality – and therefore her status as a marriageable and respectable woman. Ania Loomba has demonstrated how, from the sixteenth century onwards, black men are stereotyped as innately lascivious,[4] a stereotype which was very quick to catch on. Thomas Rymer's interpretation of *Othello* in 1693 as 'a caution to all Maidens of Quality, how, without their parents' consent they run away with Blackamoors', according to Loomba, reflects 'a patriarchal view of female waywardness and the necessity of obedience, a racist warning against the rampant sexuality of black men, and a class consciousness which prioritises the submission of women "of Quality"'.[5] Although Rymer's reading seems a far cry from those of today, alarmingly, Allan Bloom, writing in 1964, agrees with Rymer's assessment of the play:

> [From] the highest standpoint, we must come to the defence of civil society and see [Desdemona's] defection as the result of a monstrous misconception.[6]

Bloom's right-wing reading (right-wing, insofar as he draws a moral from the play, like Rymer, to 'beware of Blackamoors') implicitly sees Othello – the very thing Desdemona 'feared to look on' (I.iii.98) – as a Caliban figure. Like Othello, Caliban commits a symbolic rape of a white woman and is condemned accordingly. Caliban is an extreme version of Othello insofar as he is identified by and condemned for his unruly sexuality in his attempt to 'liberate' a white woman from the domination of her father. But Miranda, unlike Desdemona, subscribes wholeheartedly to patriarchy, and her treatment of Caliban, whom she refers to as 'Abhorred slave', is reminiscent of the hideous mythical figures – 'the cannibals that each other eat;/The Anthropophagi, and men whose heads/Do grow beneath their shoulders' (I.iii.143–4) – described by Othello in his traveller's tales. Astonishingly, Othello wins Desdemona's heart through his racist discourse; that is, her attraction to him is equated with her pleasure in listening to racist myths.

What is notable, when looking at film and televisual representations of Othello and Caliban, is that directors bend over backwards in order to suggest an anti-racist stance or try to eliminate race altogether in their screenplays. Astonishingly, Shakespeare critic Gary Taylor similarly deletes the issue of race in his comments on Othello by comparing him with O. J. Simpson. It is indeed possible to see Simpson modelling himself on Shakespeare's tragic figure: compare Simpson's suicide note, 'If we had problems it's because I loved her too much' with Othello's 'one that loved not wisely but too well'. According to Taylor, the story of O. J. Simpson, an all-American figure, former football hero, broadcaster and actor – the unusual combination of black and successful – on trial for killing his former (white) wife and friend, like *Othello*, is not a story about love. It is not a story about race, either. Race is an excuse that white men use to avoid having to face the fact that most wife-murderers are white.[7]

On the contrary, much of the story's interest derives from the fact that O. J. Simpson *is* black. And Taylor could have just as easily cited another Shakespeare play, *The Tempest*, and noticed similarities between Caliban and Simpson, concluding (as Prospero seems to) that 'savages' cannot be civilised. Barbara Ehrenreich writes in the *Guardian* of her confusion when first hearing the O. J. story:

> At first I was so clueless I confused O.J. with Jackie O – and in fact there is a certain resemblance. Struggling to explain the historical importance of O.J., the newspeople kept coming up with same content-free terms they had applied to Jackie O – 'grace', 'role model' and 'bone structure'.[8]

'Bone structure' and 'grace' are almost always applied to women, and 'role model' suggests that the rest of the race are in some way inferior – it is hard to imagine applying this set of terms to a white man and, as Ehrenreich implies, the television commentary becomes inescapably racist. Simpson has become a subject of the (white) gaze, and accordingly identified as 'Other'. In her introduction to *Race-ing Justice, Engendering Power: Essays on Anita Hill, Clarence Thomas and the Construction of Social Reality* (1993), Toni Morrison notes that in descriptions of black people, white discourse is often distinguishable from black discourse as it invariably refers to the person's body.[9] Undoubtedly the white reportage of black persons has its origins in white culture's obsession with the black body, especially with the black male organ. Reports of the O. J. Simpson trial often contradict themselves in their attempts to claim, on one hand, Simpson's 'let the side down' (successful black men have an obligation to be law-abiding) while, on the other hand, the story should be regarded as having nothing to do with race (successful black men should not be and are not distinguished from their white counterparts).

This chapter will examine how Othello and Caliban are both subject to the white gaze in filmic and critical interpretations. Othello is often 'whitened' – as in Welles's cinematic reading – through a minimal use of make-up and physical contact, while Caliban is 'blackened' by emphasising his body. The end result is a selective version of the plays, a version akin to Victorian bowdlerisation. If sex does not offend (as it did the Victorian audience/readers), racism most certainly does today. In reflecting on how Shakespeare's racist discourse is eliminated, distorted or magnified in literary criticism and in film and television representations, this chapter will attempt to answer whether or not it is possible to provide an anti-racist version of either play without distorting the text and 'whitewashing' the Bard. It seems that Shakespeare played safe in *The Tempest*, while playing with fire in *Othello* in his representation of interracial relationships. It is important to note that at the margins of the former play is the inter-racial marriage of Claribel and the King of Tunis. The marriage is read as a bad omen by the shipwrecked party. Sebastian reminds Alonso of the former disapproval of the court:

> You were kneeled to and importuned otherwise
> By all of us, and the fair soul herself
> Weighed between loathness and obedience at
> Which end o'th'beam should bow. (II.i.134–7)

We are told that Claribel ('the fair soul'), like the rest of the court, 'loathed' the marriage but in the end dutifully obeyed her father and married what Miranda calls a 'villain' which she does 'not love to look on'. Both plays seem to simultaneously confirm and question the stereotype of the lascivious black man.

Othello on Screen

Shot between 1948 and 1952 (Welles kept running out of money), *Othello* won the Grand Prix at the 1952 Cannes Film Festival. The film, shot in Mogador, Morocco and Venice, oscillates between bleak, wide-open, windswept exteriors and complex Piranesi-style interiors, making complex use of shadows (which frequently cast cagelike patterns on the actors' faces, visually reinforcing the fact that they are trapped). Suzanne Cloutier's much maligned Desdemona[10] is un-remittingly pure – she is the epitome of the self-sacrificing passive woman, especially evident in the death scene, where we see a framed picture of the Virgin Mary as a preface to the framing of Desdemona in her churchlike bedchamber. Her reclined and resigned figure is reminiscent of Renaissance paintings of the Death of the Virgin. Welles's Othello is similarly doomed and heroic. That he is predestined to fall is announced at the beginning of the film in which the end is shown. The bodies of Desdemona and Othello are carried in state and their dirge is juxtaposed with the figure of Iago, played by Micheál MacLiammóir, violently hoisted up in a cage. Welles's narrative strategy is clearly to keep the end in sight, visually calling attention to the caging or entrapment of individuals within this claustrophobic society. The film shifts our sympathies away from the tortured Iago at the commencement of the film to those who torture him at the film's closure. Welles's film ironically and complexly moves the blame away from the individual and towards the society which entraps those who step out of line.

Importantly, Iago's treacherous nature is announced in Welles's voice-over introduction; and Iago's first lines in the film – 'I have told thee often and I will retell thee again and again, I hate the Moor. I'll poison his delight' – take care of motivation problems (which have dogged much critical discussion). Rather than feel Othello and Desdemona are mismatched because of the colour of their skin, it would be more appropriate to see the mismatch in terms of age, size and personal attractiveness. Physical contact between the two is kept to the minimum, presumably to signal Desdemona's sexual innocence. The black-and-white *film noir* approach of Welles diminishes Othello's blackness – Welles's dark make-up is only just noticeable. The elimination of colour in the film is in keeping with the way the play was, on the whole, read in this period; critics of the mid-twentieth century look at the play without much consideration of race, focusing instead, like Welles, on the individual. Both William Empson and F. R. Leavis, writing on the play in the in the early 1950s, make no reference to Othello's blackness.[11] If Othello's blackness is taken into account, it is done so only in order to establish precisely what Shakespeare meant by a 'moor' and just how black Othello should be[12] rather than to contemplate Othello's amazing integration into white society.

Unlike Welles's Othello, it is impossible to avoid the issue of race when viewing Laurence Olivier's Othello (1965), directed by John Burge (based on John Dexter's National Theatre production). Heavily blacked up and employing an 'African' voice, Olivier enters wearing a dressing gown and an 'ethnic' necklace. He smugly congratulates himself on his conquest of Desdemona, like a child pleased with a new toy. Commenting on his role as Othello, Olivier remarked, 'I do not think I would dare to play the Moor as a full-blooded Negro. I play it very dark. I think Shakespeare felt a great excitement at the difference between white and black.'[13] How Olivier explores this difference in his performance is problematic indeed. Extraordinarily, the director leaves in the moment that one can't help thinking about throughout the film, when Othello's make-up comes off over Desdemona's face. She is literally and disturbingly 'blackened' when Olivier's Othello holds her dead body against his. Certainly one reviewer found the degree of colour chosen distasteful: he sees it as a huge mistake 'to make this Moor . . . blacker than black, almost blue, so as to milk (if I may be allowed to mix my colors) Othello's *negritude* for all it is worth – or, rather, for all that it isn't'.[14] The suggestion is that it would have been more palatable if Othello were only a 'little black'. Unfortunately, on video it is often difficult to see Olivier's Othello as his blackness blends in with the background; at times, only his rolling eyes are visible.

Similarly, critics of the period, in addressing Othello's blackness, unwittingly reveal their own racist attitudes. M. R. Ridley, for instance, editor of the Arden edition (first published in 1958, reprinted with corrections in 1962 and the Arden text until 1996, when it was redone by A. J. Honigmann), condemns Miss Preston's notorious account that 'Shakespeare was too correct a delineator of human nature to have coloured Othello *black* if he had personally acquainted himself with the idiosyncrasies of the African race.'[15] Instead, Ridley produces a 'liberal' reading:

> Now a good deal of the trouble arises, I think, from a confusion of colour and contour. To a great many people the word 'negro' suggests at once the picture of what they would call a 'nigger', the woolly hair, thick lips, round skull, blunt features, and burnt cork blackness of the traditional nigger minstrel. Their subconscious generalisation is as silly as that implied in Miss Preston's 'the African race' or Coleridge's 'veritable negro'. There are more races than one in Africa, and that a man is black in colour is no reason why he should, even to European eyes, look sub-human. One of the finest heads I have ever seen on any human being was that of a negro conductor on an American

Pullman car. He had lips slightly thicker than an ordinary European's, and he had somewhat curly hair; for the rest he had a long head, a magnificent forehead, a keenly chiselled nose, rather sunken cheeks, and his expression was grave, dignified, and a trifle melancholy. He was coal-black, but he might have sat to a sculptor for a statue of Caesar, or, so far as appearance went, have played a superb Othello.[16]

Ridley, perhaps like Welles, makes Othello 'white' by distinguishing him from 'the traditional nigger minstrel' by giving him European features. Extraordinarily, Olivier plays Othello as a version of the mythical 'traditional nigger minstrel' described by Ridley. Othello's frequent laughs at himself and his self-satisfied airs suggest he is not capable of the seriousness of his white associates. To a lesser extent, Anthony Hopkins (in the BBC version, 1981) falls into the same trap: blacked-up, with an uncertain and incredulous intonation in his voice, his Othello cannot cope with the sophisticated intelligent society of which he is 'privileged' to be a part. Olivier's original entry, playing childishly with a rose, is strangely imitated by Janet Suzman in her production (filmed in 1988 at the Market Theatre, Johannesburg) starring the black actor, John Kani, as Othello. Meant to be an anti-apartheid production, the filmed version of the play sends out mixed signals. When it is announced that Othello has wed a white woman, there are gasps from the crowd, clearly made to be relevant to a South African audience familiar with the banning of mixed marriages. Barbara Hodgdon has read this film as one which asks viewers 'to radically revise their racist memories',[17] culminating in Othello's symbolic castration of Iago before his own suicide, an act which, in its South African context, reverses power relations between black and white and thereby enacts the fear of white disempowerment. Unfortunately, Kani delivers the lines as if he is reading an autocue for the first time (unwittingly suggesting his inferiority), and although there is plenty of physical contact between himself and Desdemona (of which there is very little in the Welles version), emotional conviction is completely lacking. This is a physical rather than cerebral relationship; and it sends out well-meaning but ultimately racist signals in its emphasis on the body.[18]

Trevor Nunn's film of his *Othello* at Stratford's The Other Place (1989) cast black opera singer Willard White as Othello. Nunn is careful to keep most of the passion off stage but in doing so manages to push Iago (played by Ian McKellen) on to centre stage, and as one critic commented, seemingly without irony, there is 'in a subsidiary role, a particularly attractive performance from a black opera singer'.[19] White's name isn't even mentioned.

Dympna Callaghan has called attention to the use of blackface and whiteface paint in order to construct representations of blackness and femininity on the early modern stage; crucially, this calls attention to the figures as *representations*. As she points out, Desdemona ('smooth as monumental alabaster') is, of course, like Othello, a white man:

> *Othello* dramatizes the possible consequences of not excluding the racial other from the community and so presents the dazzling specta- cle of someone who is, like Caliban, both monster and man. Yet, even as it does so the play reenacts the exclusionary privilege on which such representations were founded. Othello was a white man.[20]

It was not until 1833 that Othello was played by a black actor (Ira Aldrige) on the London stage and not until 1995 that Othello was played by a black actor in a major screen production; accordingly, film representation lags substantially behind theatre in its mainte- nance of the unofficial colour bar. It is worth noting than in *Birth of a Nation* (1915), the 'black' characters were actually whites in make-up, strangely similar to the early representations of the moor on the Jacobean stage. In the more 'progressive' and arguably more influen- tial *Gone with the Wind* (1939), however, blacks were privileged to be a part of the cast, but playing the parts of racial stereotypes, dooming actresses such as Hattie McDaniel to perform the role of 'Mammy' for the rest of her career. Here the 'representation' becomes the 'real' thing, that is, the stereotype is endorsed by the presence of the black actor playing the part (who often, as in the case of Butterfly McQueen, who played 'Prissy' in *Gone with the Wind*, deeply regretted her part in perpetuating the myth of the superstitious, innately servile black child[21]); and, worryingly, this may be a key consideration in using black actors to play the parts of Shakespeare's black characters.

While critics stress that we must move from evaluating Othello as if he were 'the real thing' to, importantly, a representation of a black man, theatre and film productions insist on presenting Othello as 'really' black. Ania Loomba has contended that it is more productive to recast the plays entirely in different cultural contexts where 'we can glimpse radical changes in the relationship between the popular and high culture, the indigenous and the foreign, the original and its appropriations'.[22] However, it is more acceptable to Hollywood to cast blacks as blacks and whites as whites, trusting in the political correctness of Shakespeare.

Oliver Parker's 1995 film (released in early 1996 in the UK) with black actor Laurence Fishburne as Othello and usual good-guy Kenneth Branagh in the role of the villain, was billed as an 'erotic thriller' and, in the pre-publicity information, very little mention is made of race, even though the film features the first black man to play the role on the big screen. Yet it is difficult not to be sceptical about the reasons why this film was made so hot on the heels of the O. J. Simpson trial. Simpson's trial proved unequivocally that the representation of race is indeed highly lucrative; and at least one reviewer made the connection, commenting that 'Fishburne is exotic, proud, bald and more than usually violent, a nod perhaps to O. J. Simpson contemporaneity.'[23] In fact, on the film set, Parker was drawn into commenting on whether he had the case in mind while filming: 'impossible not to', admitted Parker. But he went on to claim that although 'there are uncanny parallels in the events . . . here we *know* Othello did it'.[24] The comparison between O. J. and Othello somehow casts Fisburne's Othello in a negative light, as a reviewer for the *L.A. Weekly* observes, 'there is something so creepy and so very O. J. in the initial love scene between Othello and Desdemona'.[25] The film discreetly but consistently calls attention to race, opening with a shot of a black man *en route* to his wedding, crossing the Grand Canal in Venice by gondola, holding a white carnival mask to his face. Although possibly alluding to the fact that in previous productions Othello wore a black mask, unsuccessfully concealing his white skin, the image disturbingly prefaces the film with the suggestion that in marrying a white woman, Othello is playing at being white himself. In casting a black actress as Bianca, Parker implies that Cassio's and Bianca's relationship is an inversion of that of the central couple; yet Parker makes clear that the black Bianca's only use is to gratify male sexual desire. The thematics of black and white are reinforced by Kenneth Branagh's Iago, who uses chess pieces of the black king and white queen to illustrate his monologues. Perversely, he triumphs as arch-manipulator: his seemingly gratuitous gesture of throwing the chess pieces into a well prefigures the ceremonial throwing of the bodies of Othello and

Desdemona into the sea at the completion of the film – in this film, Iago, played by a director, is in control right to the end.

Branagh plays Iago as a Shakespearean version of Francis Urquhart (from the TV mini-series, *House of Cards*, 1990, *To Play the King* and *The Final Cut*, 1994); his addresses to the camera, like those of Urquhart, assume a naughty complicity with the audience. We are, perhaps unintentionally, invited to applaud his ingenuity as he comes across as the most attractive figure in the film. Certainly this is the opinion of the reviewer in the *Evening Standard*, who begins by complaining about Othello's blackness: 'Fishburne's blackness, in terms of Shakespeare's play, is the wrong shade. It is ghetto blackness. It is associated with Hollywood's "blax-ploitation" factory, not the Doge of Venice's military hierarchy.'[26] The review concludes that, unsurprisingly, Fishburne's Othello 'is the first Othello . . . who actually looks shiftier than Iago'.[27] Reviews are virtually unanimous in disliking Irene Jacob's Desdemona for being foreign and xenophobia – again, probably unintentionally – creeps into the film as well. The only one who goes down well with the reviewers is the quintessentially British Kenneth Branagh.

Like Suzman, Parker calls attention to Othello's sexuality in the depiction of his relationship with Desdemona (likened to a 'kitschy soft-porn Emmanuelle movie',[28] 'just explicit enough to garner an R rating'[29]) and by visualising Othello's nightmare vision of Cassio and Desdemona's sexual encounters. This is an Othello who is violent and overtly sexual in orientation; the film, in its emphasis on Othello's body, alarmingly, reinforces a racial stereotype and, as in the case of O. J. Simpson, is ultimately exploitative in its representation of race.

Welles in the 1950s decides to ignore race, Burge (and Dexter) in the 1960s, reproduce a racial stereotype and Parker in the 1990s inserts images to underline the racist themes in the play, images which perhaps pander to his audience's obsession with race. The last film, in its use of a black actor in the title part, may be the most racist of all.

The Tempest on Screen

Othello as a film will, perhaps, always be problematic – the leading role inevitably will cause difficulties with directors. *The Tempest* is another matter altogether – the representation of Caliban is surpris-

ingly unproblematic in the latter half of this century, as evidenced in
two major film releases, Derek Jarman's *The Tempest* and Peter
Greenaway's *Prospero's Books*. Caliban the 'thing of darkness',
although not explicitly black, undoubtedly is represented with what
Homi Bhabha calls 'those terrifying stereotypes of savagery, cannibal-
ism, lust and anarchy which are the signal points of identification,
scenes of fear and desire'.[30]

In Act I, Scene ii, the major *dramatis personae* of the play appear.
Briefly, Miranda asks about the tempest, Prospero answers her and
fills her in with aspects of her history which have formerly been
concealed from her and then puts her to sleep. Ariel arrives and
Prospero similarly bullies him by reminding him of his own history
when he was cruelly tortured by the witch Sycorax. After this Ariel
leaves, Miranda awakes and Caliban enters. Caliban gives his own
record of the past and declares his right to the island which Prospero
rejects – he reminds Caliban that he was a part of their household
until he tried to rape Miranda. Caliban leaves and Ferdinand enters,
whereupon Miranda sees him and instantly falls in love. It is worth
looking at these two 'courtships' together.

Prospero	Thou most lying slave,
	Whom stripes may move, not kindness! I have used thee,
	Filth as thou art, with human care; and lodged thee
	In mine own cell, till thou didst seek to violate
	The honour of my child.
Caliban	O ho, O ho! Would't had been done!
	Thou didst prevent me; I had peopled else
	This isle with Calibans. (I.ii.347–53)
Ferdinand	Most sure the goddess
	On whom these airs attend. Vouchsafe my prayer
	May know if you remain upon this island,
	And that you will some good instruction give
	How I may bear me here. My prime request,
	Which I do last pronounce, is – O you wonder –
	If you be maid or no? (I.ii.423–9)
	O, if a virgin,
	And your affection not gone forth, I'll make you
	The Queen of Naples. (450–52)

The question we need to ask is, why does Ferdinand succeed where Caliban fails? Within seconds of meeting her, he asks her about her sexual status and then, with indecent haste, he asks her to be his wife. What is the difference between Caliban's and Ferdinand's language and situations? It has been the custom to regard Caliban as inhuman, an alien, like the supernatural force in the science-fiction adaptation, *Forbidden Planet* (1956; directed by Fred Wilcox, starring Walter Pidgeon, Anne Francis and Leslie Nielsen). Here Caliban is 'a monster from the Id', risen from the mind of the Prospero character in the film; uniquely, Prospero is made responsible for this destructive force.

A more 'standard' reading of Caliban is offered by Frank Kermode in the Arden edition of the text:

> If Aristotle was right in arguing that 'men . . . who are as much inferior to others as the body is to the soul . . . are slaves by nature . . . then, the black and mutilated cannibal must be the natural slave of the European gentleman, and . . . the salvage and deformed Caliban of the learned Prospero.
>
> . . . [Caliban's] origins and character are natural in the sense that they do not partake of grace, civility, and art; he is ugly in body, associated with an evil natural magic, and unqualified for rule or nurture. He exists at the simplest level of sensual pain and pleasure, fit for lechery because love is beyond his nature, and a natural slave of demons.[31]

Kermode sees Caliban as unproblematically evil; give him too much scope and he will reveal his bestiality by raping Miranda. As he is more a beast than a man, he is by necessity oversexed. And his bestiality is reflected in his appearance, reinforced by the 1979 cover of the edition which portrays a Darwinian ape/man with threatening hands/claws emerging from beneath a tree trunk. What is interesting in Kermode's account is that the stereotype is not questioned but taken for granted. At worst, Kermode's interpretation is itself making cultural assumptions about Caliban which today smack of racism. At best, he offers a view of the play which sees Shakespeare as a product of a racist society.

Kermode's reading coincides with the standard 'safe' reading provided by John Gorrie's BBC production of 1980. Warren Clarke plays Caliban in a simple, undemanding reading of the play. Like

Kermode's reading, Caliban is made subhuman, seemingly in order to avoid questions about racial and cultural differences in the play. This representation is one for Animal Rights campaigners to take on board. He is made literally into a beast – strangely resembling a gigantic puppy at Prospero's feet (and at the foot of the screen) – apparently in order to justify Prospero's harsh treatment of him. However, Prospero, played by Michael Hordern, keeps his distance visually – there is no violence towards Caliban as suggested by the language (whenever Prospero speaks to Caliban, he is abusive, addressing him as 'filth', 'poisonous slave' and 'lying Slave'); in this version, there is no attempt to give the words visual correlatives.

A much more progressive reading of the play is provided a year earlier than the BBC production by Derek Jarman. *The Tempest*, subtitled 'as seen through the eyes of Derek Jarman', is set in the deserted Georgian wing of the Tudor house, Stoneleigh Abbey in Warwickshire, and was also filmed on the Northumberland coastline. The *dramatis personae* take refuge in the neglected house, like victims of a holocaust. Prospero, played by Heathcote Williams, half the age of all previous Prosperos, and Miranda, played by Toyah Wilcox, shocked the original audience as they were not the sorts to perform Shakespeare; as Jarman himself reports, the Americans especially disapproved of his 'messing with "Will Shakespeare"' – 'The Anglo-Saxon tradition has to be defended; and putting my scissors in was like an axe-blow to the last redwood.'[32] The AA/15 rating of the film is largely due to the obscene behaviour of Caliban, played by Jack Birkett. Interestingly, he is a human being (not subhuman, as in the BBC version), represented as non-threatening, old, decrepit, stupid and gay. If Jarman's own homosexuality was not so well known, this could be interpreted as an anti-gay production.[33] This Caliban is a different kind of outsider, ultimately pathetic rather than contemptible. As Jarman himself complained, the film vexed traditionalists as it was not regarded as authentic Shakespeare (even though all the lines, except for the final song, *Stormy Weather*, are Shakespeare's) – it was not, like the BBC version, what we have come to expect of the play.

Importantly, Caliban was portrayed as human – and, although the abuse towards him was underplayed, the film highlights the undeserved privileges of the rest of the cast. Jarman toyed with the idea of a black Caliban but rejected it 'because I thought it would load the whole film in one way, make it more specific than general'.[34] It has been suggested that Jack Birkett has 'Afro-Caribbean' features,[35] but this is hardly perceptible and thus cannot allow for a racialised reading of Caliban. In the film, Caliban's mother Sycorax is undeniably white and Birkett's Caliban is only distinguished physically from the rest of the cast through his bulk and his exaggerated expressions. Jarman did include two blacks in his cast – the King of Tunis, married to Claribel, and Elisabeth Welch, who sings 'Stormy Weather' at the end of the film. Although Elisabeth Welch's presence is both witty and liberating, Jarman visualises the oft-forgotten marriage of Claribel and the King of Tunis in a scene suggesting Tunis's domination over and corruption of the white Claribel. The image is unsettling; briefly suggesting underlying racial tensions.

Six years after Jarman's film, Paul Brown's "'This thing of darkness I acknowledge mine": *The Tempest* and the discourse of colonialism' (in *Political Shakespeare*, ed. Jonathan Dollimore and Alan Sinfield) looks at Caliban as a victim of Prospero's colonisation and Caliban as a representative of the indigenous population. Prospero forges a history for himself and Caliban in which he can justify the latter's enslavement. So, Brown explains, Miranda is 'represented' as wronged virgin ' to be protected from the rapist native and presented to a civil lover, Ferdinand. . . . Prospero's narrative can be seen, then, to operate as a reality principle, ordering and correcting the inhabitants of the island, subordinating their discourse to his own.'[36] The history of Caliban and Prospero is a miniature version of white colonial history: white man arrives, the natives are initially friendly and show them the features of the new land; in turn, the white man attempts to educate the native; and the native ultimately reveals in some way his 'bestiality' and as a result is put down, either enslaved or destroyed by the white man who righteously takes possession of the territory.

Brown's reading of the play has been extremely influential. John Salway, for instance, in 1989, reads *The Tempest* as a reworking of *Othello*, concerned with the representation of the 'other' or the racial outsider in Shakespeare:

> Comparing *The Tempest* with *Othello* suggests some interesting parallels. As Caliban is lodged in Prospero's own cell, so Othello is admitted into the very bosom of European culture. Here, too, the

privileged alien is seen getting uppity and trying to seduce a white girl. In both cases, the girl's father sees this as a violation of honour.[37]

He sees Caliban as being created by white paranoia, and what is interesting about the play, for him, is that Caliban's actions constantly contradict Prospero's narrative. Stephen Orgel, similarly, sees this conflict as crucial to the representation of authority in the play:

> Caliban's accusations against Prospero of usurpation and enslavement reveal an unexpected solidity. Few Renaissance theorists considered the claims of native populations seriously, and Prospero does not undertake to refute Caliban's charges. He assumes his authority, and rules by virtue of his ability to do so. But precisely for that reason the question of authority – on the island, or in any state – remains open.[38]

Caliban's oppositional voice, or what Martin Orkin describes as 'the courage of Caliban's intellectual will to resist throughout',[39] is amazingly ignored by Peter Greenaway's reactionary reading of the play, in which Caliban is dwarfed by an omnipotent Prospero.

In 1991, Peter Greenaway made his contribution to the Shakespeare-on-screen canon with his version of *The Tempest*, *Prospero's Books*. The film, which uses computer-generated imagery, is set in a palazzo, with most of the lines spoken by John Gielgud who plays the part of Prospero. In fact, the solipsistic world created by Prospero is not far removed from Jarman's version – Jarman had previously talked with Gielgud about playing Prospero and in 1975 had drawn up plans in which a mad Prospero played all the parts.[40] Greenaway's film departs radically from the play text in its use of a series of volumes which come alive on screen: the final book, 'A book of 35 Plays with room for one more', is the final volume mentioned. At the end of the film, the thirty-sixth book, *The Tempest*, is included in the volume, and living up to his promise, Prospero throws all the books into the water. The last two books are fished out by Caliban. The first of these is Shakespeare's *First Folio* (with room for one more play), the second is a fresh copy of *The Tempest*, a fictional Shakespearean holograph.

The spirits of Prospero's island, together with Caliban, are distinguished from the court party as they are naked, the latter clothed in extravagantly uncomfortable costumes. Caliban enters the film by slashing, urinating and defecating on Prospero's books. Played by the avant-garde dancer, Michael Clark, Caliban communicates through dancing – his movements suggest his primitivism, which could be either the result of nature or nurture.[41] Prospero keeps his distance from Caliban throughout, and there is no physical abuse, let alone contact between the two – in fact, Gielgud remarked that they never actually met during the filming.[42] The nudity of Caliban invariably links him with the other manifold naked spirits, and as one reviewer noted, the nudity is not employed as a celebration of the body, but rather invokes shades of Nazi concentration camps.[43] Significantly, Caliban is white as Greenaway seems to have ignored recent developments in criticism of *The Tempest* in this production. As in Jarman's *Tempest*, a possible faint allusion to the Holocaust[44] and the marriage of the King of Tunis to Claribel are visualised. Claribel is depicted, post-penetration, her abdomen covered in blood, while her black husband is being washed down by servants. This moment in the film seems to confirm, unproblematically, the potential racism of the play and it demonstrates that to show something is different from writing about it – it is easy to suggest that the play calls attention to racial differences, but to visualise this is a different matter. For this reason, Caliban is presented as white by Greenaway.

Films of *Othello* and *The Tempest* are problematic when screened as they unfortunately date so quickly. Olivier blacked up and hamming it up as a racial stereotype is shockingly racist when viewed now. Even the likes of Peter Greenaway and Derek Jarman censor the potential racism of Shakespeare and in doing so unwittingly participate in a revised form of Victorian bardolatry, censoring race rather than sex, creating their own versions of 'Family Shakespeare'.

To quote John Collick, 'film companies rarely make a movie out of a Shakespeare play simply because they're short of material. There are very definite reasons for reproducing the plays and the tradition to which they belong.'[45] Clearly Parker's film capitalises on a 1990s obsession with the portrayal of race, ultimately revealing how apparently anti-racist readings are doomed to be racist. It is perhaps now too difficult to evade the issue of race in *Othello* and produce a filmed version of the 'lascivious moor' without causing offence; and it is surprising that *The Tempest* can so recently inspire films which are, as Derek Jarman has pronounced, 'an island of the mind'.[46] But this 'island of the mind' is not seamless: a careful reading of these films reveals unresolved racial tensions.

The Texts – *Othello,* I.iii.47–293

A comparison of Orson Welles's 1952 version of the attack and self-defence of Othello (I.iii.47–293) with Oliver Parker's (1995) shows Welles's Othello to be much more dominant; whereas Parker gives more space to the other *dramatis personae*. While Welles's text is by far the most slimmed down (he retains less that a third while the Parker version keeps just over half), Othello is still allowed about half of the original lines. (Compare this to Desdemona in Welles's film who keeps about one-third, while Parker's Desdemona keeps approximately four-fifths of her lines.) While both versions indicate that Othello has swayed his audience, Welles chooses to retain the Duke's observation, 'I think this tale would win my daughter too' whereas Parker keeps the Duke's final comments to Brabantio: 'If virtue no delighted beauty lack/ Your son-in-law is far more fair than black.' Interestingly, Parker chooses the compliment to Othello which has obvious racist overtones.

While Welles's Othello is always seen as (literally) head and shoulders above the rest of the cast, Parker's Othello is seen from a variety of angles, revealing his whole body. In fact, during the 'Her father lov'd me' speech, Parker inserts flashbacks which call into question Othello's assertion that Desdemona loved him for the 'dangers pass'd'. We follow her gaze as she clearly is attracted to his body (rather than what he has to say). Parker's shooting script contains further flashbacks illustrating the story of Othello's life from youth to manhood, including a young Othello fending off a group of attackers with a bone.[47] (It is probable that they were removed as they overstated Othello's position as 'alien' or 'other'.)

What is missing from both adaptations is the remarkable power struggle between Brabantio, Othello and Desdemona in which they compete to finish each other's lines. For example, when the Duke proposes that Desdemona should stay in her father's house, all three are quick off the mark:

Brabantio   I'll not have it so.

Othello   Nor I.
Desdemona   Nor I. I would not there reside. (I.iii.240–3)

It is Desdemona who gets her way. In fact, Othello asks that she be given the supreme power in the dispute, asking the Duke to 'Let her have your voice' (line 260). Desdemona's self-assertion is also self-obsession. Her first speech is remarkable in its reiteration of 'I', 'me' and 'my' and the way in which she positions everything or everyone in relation to herself: 'my noble father', 'my life and education', 'my duty', 'my husband' and 'my mother'. Her self-obsession-assertion is clearly threatening to both father and husband; and the scene changes subtly from an attack on race to an attack on gender. Brabantio's hatred of Othello is ultimately exchanged for hatred of his daughter, siding with Othello as he exits the scene, 'She has deceiv'd her father, and may thee.' The following text is based on Peter Alexander's edition (1951) and the words as they appear on the soundtracks; Welles's inclusions are in bold, Parker's are underlined. Interpolations are indicated on the right-hand side in brackets when they occur at the end of a line, and within the text in brackets if they occur within the line.

Enter BRABANTIO, OTHELLO, IAGO, RODERIGO, and Officers

1 Senator   **Here comes** Brabantio and **the** valiant **Moor.**
Duke   <u>Valiant Othello, we must straight employ you</u>
                <u>Against the general</u> enemy Ottoman.[<u>Turkish foe</u>]
                [*To Brabantio*] I did not see you; <u>welcome,
                    gentle signior;</u>
                <u>We lack'd your counsel and your help tonight.</u>
Brabantio   <u>So did I yours. Good</u> **your Grace**<u>, pardon me</u>:
                          [*Repeated*: **your grace**]
                <u>Neither my place, nor aught I heard of business,</u>
                Hath [<u>Has</u>] rais'd me from my bed; nor doth the general
                    care
                Take hold on me; for my particular grief
                Is of so flood-gate and o'erbearing nature   10
                That it engluts and swallows other sorrows,
                And it is still itself.
Duke   [**Brabantio**]

Why, **what's the matter?**

Brabantio   **My daughter! O, my daughter!**

All   Dead?

Brabantio   Ay, to me.

She is abus'd, stol'n from me, and [ay] **corrupted,** [by magic spells.

By spells and medicines brought of mountebanks;
For nature so preposterously to err,
Being not deficient, blind, or lame of sense,
Sans witchcraft could not.

Duke: Whoe'er he be that in this foul proceeding
Hath thus beguil'd your daughter of herself,
And you of her, the bloody book of law
You shall yourself read in the bitter letter

If she in chains of magic was not bound/ Whether a maid, so tender, fair and happy./ Would ever have, to incur a general mock,/ Run from her father [*changed from 'guardage'*] **to the sooty bosom/Of such a thing as that** [*changed from 'thou'*]**?/Damned as thou art, thou has enchanted her.**] [*Text transposed from I.ii. 63–71*]

After your own sense; yea, though our proper son
Stood in your action.

Brabantio   Humbly I thank your Grace.
Here is the man – this Moor whom now, it seems,
Your special mandate for the state affairs
Hath hither brought.

All   We are very sorry for't.

Duke [To Othello]   [**Othello**]
What, in your own part, can you say to this?   30

Brabantio   **Nothing, but this is so.**   [*Move to ll. 66–8 (Welles's version) and return to l.32 (this text)*]

Othello   **Most potent, grave, and reverend signiors,**
My very noble and approv'd good masters:
That I have ta'en away this old man's daughter,
It is most true; true, I have married her -
The very head and front of my offending
Hath this extent, no more. Rude am I in my speech,
And little blest with the soft phrase of peace;
For since these arms of mine had seven years' pith,

Till now some nine moons wasted, they have us'd   40
Their dearest action in the tented field;
And little of this great world can I speak
More than pertains to feats of broil and battle;
And therefore little can [shall] I grace my cause
In speaking for myself. Yet, by your gracious patience,
I will a round unvarnish'd tale deliver
Of my whole course of love – what drugs, what charms,
What conjuration, and what mighty magic,
For such proceedings am I charg'd withal,
I won his daughter.

Brabantio   A maiden never bold,   50
Of spirit so still and quiet that her motion
Blush'd at herself; and she – in spite of nature,
Of years, of country, credit, every thing –
To fall in love with what she fear'd to look on!
It is a judgment maim'd and most imperfect
That will confess perfection so could err
Against all rules of nature, and must be driven
To find out practices of cunning hell,
Why this should be. I therefore vouch again
That with some mixtures powerful o'er the blood,   60
Or with some dram conjur'd to this effect,
He wrought upon her.

Duke   To vouch this is no proof –
Without more wider and more overt test
Than these thin habits and poor likelihoods
Of modern seeming do prefer against him.

1 Senator   But, **Othello**, speak.
Did you by indirect and forced courses
Subdue and poison this young maid's affections?
Or came it by request, and such fair question
As soul to soul affordeth?

Othello   I do beseech you,   70
Send for the lady to the Sagittary,
And let her speak of me before her father.
If you do find me foul in her report,
The trust, the office, I do hold of you
Not only take away, but let your sentence

	Even fall upon my life.	
Duke	Fetch Desdemona hither.	
Othello	Ancient, conduct them; you best know the place.	

[*Exeunt Iago and Attendants*]

And, till she come, as faithful as to heaven
I do confess the vices of my blood,
So justly to your grave ears I'll present   80
How I did thrive in this fair lady's love,
And she in mine.

Duke	Say it, Othello.
Othello	[**Brabantio**]

Her father **lov'd me, oft invited me;**
Still question'd me the story of my life
From year to year – the battles, sieges, fortunes,
That I have pass'd.
I ran it through, **even from my boyish days**
To th' very moment that he bade me tell it;
Wherein I spake [spoke] **of most disastrous chances,**
Of moving accidents by flood and field;   90
Of **hairbreadth scapes i' th' imminent deadly breach;**
Of **being taken by the insolent foe**
And sold to slavery; of my redemption thence,
And portance in my travel's history;
Wherein of antres vast and deserts idle,
Rough quarries, rocks, and hills whose heads touch
    heaven,
It was my hint to speak – such was the process;
And of the Cannibals that each other eat,
The Anthropophagi, and men whose heads
Do grow beneath their shoulders. **This to hear**

[These things to hear]   100

Would Desdemona seriously incline;
But still the house affairs would draw her thence;
Which ever as she could with haste dispatch,
She'd come again, **and with a greedy ear**
Devour up my discourse. Which I observing,
Took once a pliant hour, and **found good means**
To draw from her a prayer of earnest heart
That [which] **I would all my pilgrimage dilate,**

Whereof by parcels she had something heard,
But not intentively. I did consent,   110
And often did beguile her of her tears,
When I did speak of some distressful stroke
That my youth suffer'd. My story being done,
<u>She gave me for my pains a world of sighs;</u>
<u>She swore, in faith, 'twas strange, 'twas passing</u>
   <u>strange;</u>
<u>'Twas pitiful, 'twas wondrous pitiful.</u>
She wish'd she had not heard it; yet she wish'd
That heaven had made her such a man.
   She thank'd me;
And [she] bade me, if I had a friend that lov'd her,
I should but teach him how to tell my story,   120
And that would woo her. Upon this hint I spake;
<u>She lov'd me for the dangers I had pass'd;</u>
<u>And I lov'd her that she did pity them.</u>
<u>This only is the witchcraft I have us'd.</u>
Here comes the lady; let her witness it.
   Enter DESDEMONA, IAGO, *and* ATTENDANTS
Duke   **I think this tale would win my daughter too.**
Good Brabantio,
Take up this mangled matter at the best.
Men do their broken weapons rather use
Than their bare hands.
Brabantio   I pray you hear her speak.   130
If she confess that she was half the wooer,
Destruction on my head if my bad blame
Light on the man! **Come hither**, gentle mistress.
           [**Desdemona**]
<u>Do you perceive in all this</u> noble <u>company</u>
<u>Where most you owe obedience?</u>
Desdemona   <u>My noble father,</u>
I do perceive here a divided duty:
<u>To you I am bound for life and education;</u>
<u>My life and education both do learn me</u>
<u>How to respect you; you are the lord of</u> all my duty -
<u>I am hitherto your daughter; but here's my</u>
   <u>husband,</u>   140

<u>**And so much duty as my mother show'd**</u>
<u>**To you, preferring you before her father,**</u>
<u>**So much I challenge that I may profess**</u>
<u>**Due to the Moor, my lord.**</u>

Brabantio   <u>Good bu'y, **I ha done**</u>.
[**God be with you, I have done.**]
Please it your Grace, on to the state affairs –
<u>I had rather to adopt a child than get it.</u>
<u>Come hither, Moor:</u>
<u>I here do give thee that with all my heart</u>
<u>Which, but thou hast already, with all my heart</u>
<u>I would keep from thee.</u> For your sake, jewel,
I am glad at soul I have no other child;
For thy escape would teach me tyranny,   150
To hang clogs on them. I have done, my lord.

Duke   Let me speak like yourself, and lay a sentence
Which, as a grise or step, may help these lovers
Into your favour.
When remedies are past, the griefs are ended
By seeing the worst, which late on hopes depended.
To mourn a mischief that is past and gone
Is the next way to draw new mischief on.
What cannot be preserv'd when fortune takes,
Patience her injury a mockery makes.   160
The robb'd that smiles steals something from the thief;
He robs himself that spends a bootless grief.

Brabantio   So let the Turk of Cyprus us beguile: [**Please it your**
We lose it not so long as we can   **Grace onto the**
    smile.   **state affairs.**]
He bears the sentence well that
    nothing bears
But the free comfort which from thence he hears;
But he bears both the sentence and the sorrow
That to pay grief must of poor patience borrow.
These sentences, to sugar or to gall,
Being strong on both sides, are equivocal.   170
But words are words: I never yet did hear
That the bruis'd heart was pierced through the ear.
<u>I humbly beseech you proceed to th'affairs of state.</u>

Duke	**The Turk with a most mighty preparation makes for Cyprus. Othello,**] [*insert* 'Th'affair cries haste, And speed must answer it' *ll. 276–7*] **the fortitude of the place is best known to you;** [*insert* **You must away this [morning]** tonight.
	[*Othello:* **With all my heart.** (*from l. 278*)] **When we consider the importancy of Cyprus to the Turk . . .** *FADE OUT*] and though we have there a substitute of most allowed sufficiency, yet opinion, a sovereign mistress of effects, throws a more safer voice on you. You must therefore be content to slubber the gloss of your new fortunes with this more stubborn and boisterous expedition.
Othello	The tyrant custom, most grave senators,
	Hath made the flinty and steel couch of war 180
	My thrice-driven bed of down. I do agnize
	A natural and prompt alacrity
	I find in hardness; and would undertake
	This present war against the Ottomites.
	Most humbly, therefore, bending to your state,
	I crave fit disposition for my wife;
	Due reference of place and exhibition;
	With such accommodation and besort
	As levels with her breeding.
Duke	If you please,
	Be't at her father's. 190
Brabantio	I'll not have it so.
Othello	Nor I.
Desdemona	Nor I. I would not there reside,
	To put my father in impatient thoughts
	By being in his eye. Most gracious Duke,
	To my unfolding lend your prosperous ear,
	And let me find a charter in your voice
	T'assist my simpleness.
Duke	What would you, Desdemona?
Desdemona	That I did love the Moor to live with him,
	My downright violence and storm of fortunes
	[scorn *for 'storm' from Q1*]
	May trumpet to the world. My heart's subdu'd 200
	Even to the utmost pleasure of my lord:

<u>I saw Othello's visage in his mind;</u>
<u>And to his honours and his valiant parts</u>
<u>Did I my soul and fortunes consecrate.</u>
<u>So that, dear lords, if I be left behind,</u>
<u>A moth of peace, and he go to the war,</u>
<u>The rites for why I love him are bereft me,</u>
<u>And I a heavy interim shall support</u>
<u>By his dear absence. Let me go with him.</u>

Othello	<u>Let her have your voice.</u>	210

Vouch with me, heaven, I therefore beg it not
To please the palate of my appetite;
Nor to comply with heat – the young affects
In me defunct – and proper satisfaction;
But to be free and bounteous to her mind.
<u>And heaven defend your good souls that you think</u>
<u>I will your serious and great business scant</u>
<u>For she is with me.</u> No, when light-wing'd toys
Of feather'd Cupid seel with wanton dullness
My speculative and offic'd instruments,   220
That my disports corrupt and taint my business,
Let huswives make a skillet of my helm,
And all indign and base adversities
Make head against my estimation!

Duke   <u>Be it as you shall privately determine,</u>
Either for her stay or going. Th'affair cries haste,
And speed must answer it. You must away to-night.

Desdemona   To-night, my lord!
Duke   This night.
Othello   With all my heart.
Duke   <u>At nine i' th' morning here we'll meet again.</u>
Othello, leave some officer behind,   230
And he shall our commission bring to you;
With such things else of quality and respect
As doth import you.

Othello   So please your Grace, my ancient;
A man he is of honesty and trust.
To his conveyance I assign my wife,
With what else needful your good Grace shall think
To be sent after me.

Duke	Let it be so.
	Good night to every one. [*To Brabantio*] 240
	And, noble signior,
	If virtue no delighted beauty lack,
	Your son-in-law is far more fair than black.
1 Senator	Adieu, brave Moor; use Desdemona well.
Brabantio	**Look to her, Moor, if thou hast eyes to see:**
	She has deceiv'd her father, and may thee.

5 Shakespeare, Film and Nationalism: *Henry V*

It is difficult to ignore the name of Kenneth Branagh in recent discussions of Shakespeare on screen; indeed, he is credited with inspiring the current wave of film adaptations with his production of *Henry V*, a film which initiated the comparisons drawn between himself and the other big name in the Shakespeare-on-screen industry – Laurence Olivier – a comparison he allegedly shuns. Oliver Parker's *Othello* (1995), Richard Loncraine's *Richard III* (1995), Trevor Nunn's *Twelfth Night* (1996), Adrian Noble's *A Midsummer Night's Dream* (1996), Baz Luhrmann's *William Shakespeare's Romeo + Juliet* (1996), Kenneth Branagh's *Hamlet* (1996) and Michael Hoffman's *A Midsummer Night's Dream* (1999), with a cast which includes Kevin Kline, Michelle Pfeiffer, Rupert Everett, Christian Bale and John Sessions have all been released in the last five years of the twentieth century. Inevitably, discussions of these films involve comparisons with their predecessors; and, similarly, the Shakespeare-on-screen phenomenon of the 1990s is considered in relation to the golden age of the 1940s and 1950s.[1] If we see Branagh as, in many respects, responsible for the current revival of interest in Shakespeare on screen, then it is worth exploring how far he departs from and how much he copies Olivier's cinematic successes.

Laurence Olivier's *Henry V*[2]

Few dispute the impression that Laurence Olivier's *Henry V* is clear-cut propaganda; filmed from June 1943 to July 1944 and premièred in

London on 22 November 1944, the film appropriates Shakespeare in order to glorify war in a morale-boosting exercise.[3] John Collick, for example, remarks that the film 'supported the mythical idea of a wholly integrated British literary culture in which Shakespeare was as meaningful to the masses as the songs of Vera Lynn'.[4]

Graham Holderness has illustrated how, in the 1940s, Wilson Knight's *Olive and the Sword* and E. M. W. Tillyard's *Shakespeare's History Plays* pay homage to what they regard as Shakespeare's vision of national unity. According to Holderness, 'their real ideological commitment . . . was only indirectly to the order of a vanished historical state, and directly to the political and ideological problems of Britain in the late 1930s and 1940s'.[5] During the war and in the postwar period, Shakespeare criticism can be seen to reflect a society afraid of change, reflected in a nostalgic desire for a natural hierarchical order as described by Shakespeare. Wilson Knight identifies a 'need' for Shakespeare. According to Knight, writing in 1943, 'we need expect no Messiah, but we might, at this hour, turn to Shakespeare, a national prophet if ever there was one, concerned deeply with the royal soul of England'. Knight regards Henry, without irony, as a 'Christian warrior'.[6]

However, during the war years and immediately afterwards, criticism of *Henry V* tends to be more negative than positive. Tillyard confidently remarks that the play is flawed because:

> In *Henry IV* Shakespeare had successfully depicted in the Prince the true kingly type, but not the ideal reigning King; in *Henry V* he failed to make interesting or consistent what should have been the perfect king in action. He had still to come to terms with that figure . . . . Shakespeare was far too sane and lived in far too perilous a world to underestimate the public and active virtues.[7]

In short, the play does not sustain the political order which Tillyard sees as the essence of Shakespeare. Mark Van Doren, writing in the United States in 1939, argues that the heroic idea is splintered, not unified, and Shakespeare himself, aware of his own artistic failure, accordingly begins the play with an apology. He remarks that '*Henry IV* . . . both was and is a successful play; it answers the questions it raises . . . it is remembered as fabulously rich and at the same time simply ordered. *Henry V* is no such play. It has its splendours and its secondary attractions, but the forces in it are not unified.'[8] Derek Traversi, writing for the journal *Scrutiny* in 1941, sees the necessity of defending the play against its critics; as an epic play, it 'demands in the monarch an impersonality which is almost tragic'.[9] The *Scrutiny* writers of the war years take issue with Tillyard's notion of order; instead, order is found in what Traversi later defines as Shakespeare's humanism, his 'concern for permanent human values'.[10] After the war, Una Ellis Fermor remarks that there is little pleasure to be had from this play and that the picture of the 'statesman king' (a description of Henry which must have had a Churchillian resonance for her readership) is not sustained as carefully as it should have been.[11] What is revealing is that the myth of Henry V and the myth of Shakespeare in the 1930s and 1940s were too sacrosanct for readers to consider Shakespeare's diminishment of Henry's heroism; and that the play simultaneously attracted and repelled in its portrayal of England's 'finest hour'.

Within such a critical context, sponsored by the Ministry of Information, Laurence Olivier eliminates half of the play's lines (most notably, episodes which cast doubt on Henry's motives and heroism) and produces the unity which critics had found missing. To achieve this, he excludes the treatment of the traitors, the speech before Harfleur in which Henry pictures the consequences of war, Henry's exchange of gloves with Williams, Henry's acknowledgement of his father's guilt in the prayer before battle, the hanging of Bardolph, the order to slay the prisoners, Henry's bawdy exchanges with Burgundy and Katherine, and the final remarks of the Chorus who reminds the audience of the ephemeral nature of Henry's victory. With the film's dedication 'To the Commandos and Airborne Troops of Great Britain, the spirit of our Ancestors', it is hard not to view the transformation of the Chorus's speeches to voice-over as evocative of a wartime correspondent describing through newsreel coverage the events leading up to the victory of D-Day.

Until Olivier's *Henry V*, Shakespeare scholarship tended to dismiss Shakespeare on film as it popularised through reduction and trivialisation of the play texts.[12] Olivier changed (or rewrote) the play for both propaganda effects and as an answer to literary critics of the film. He defended his decisions by claiming later: 'I had a mission . . . My country was at war; I felt Shakespeare within me, I felt the cinema within him.'[13] With Shakespeare's implicit permission, he 'improves' the play. Olivier chooses to retain the Chorus, but rather than representing him as Britannia or Clio, the muse of history, as had been the custom in the nineteenth century, Olivier's Chorus begins as an actor with the Lord Chamberlain's Men at the Globe Theatre in 1600. After the initial scene of the play, the Chorus directs our attention to a painted curtain depicting the coast of Southampton, and guides us from what Jorgens calls the theatrical mode to the realistic mode[14] and full (and expensive) Technicolor combined with William Walton's triumphant musical orchestration. The passage through the painted curtain, transporting us from 1600 to 1415 (and the painted scenery designed by Lindegaard, which is based on Pol de Limbourg's illuminations in *Les Tres Riches Heures*),[15] is like the movement of Dorothy from Kansas to Oz in 1939 (from black and white to colour accompanied by George Stoll's similarly phantasmagoric music). Indeed, Henry's climactic arrival at the fairy-tale-like palace of the French King in Act V clearly echoes Dorothy's arrival in Emerald City. The comparison to *The Wizard of Oz* is pertinent, as the audience, like the evacuees of war in C. S. Lewis's *The Lion, the Witch and the Wardrobe*, are allowed to escape into another world, a world of colour and excitement, in which the wooden acting of Olivier's Henry, the actor on the stage, is metamorphosed into a 'real' statesman king whose inspirational rhetoric must be seen as a tribute to Churchill during the Blitz. Clearly, Henry's speeches would remind a contemporary audience of Churchill (compare Henry's 'We few, we happy few, we band of brothers', IV.iii.60, to Churchill's 'Never in the field of human conflict was so much owed by so many to so few'). Olivier not only 'improves' upon Shakespeare's text, but he also 'improves' history itself; Churchill is transformed into a Hollywood heart-throb. In fact, Olivier has consolidated Henry into an ideological force, very much in the spirit of Wilson Knight's and Tillyard's Shakespearean criticism, which regards Shakespeare as the spokesman of national unity. James Agee's tribute to the film in 1946 testifies to the fact that Olivier's production worked as both political propaganda and legitimisation for the filming of Shakespeare:

> I was persuaded, and in part still am, that every time and place has since been in decline save one, in which one Englishman used language better than anyone has before or since . . . and that some of us are still capable of paying homage to the fact.[16]

Agee endorses the film as 'authentic' Shakespeare, significantly with no reference to Olivier's omissions and changes. Agee, as representative of Shakespeare critic and film spectator, has himself been transported through the painted curtain, from the staid world of theatre to the active and more colourful world of film.

Undoubtedly, one of the most significant deletions is the ending, in which the Chorus relates the short-lived nature of Henry's triumph, and we are led to believe that Katherine and Henry, in the tradition of romantic comedy, will persevere happily into the future. This is a marriage of past and present, film and theatre, albeit a distortion of Shakespeare's jaundiced portrait of Henry in which the sexual conquest (or rape) of Katherine is compared to his conquest of France. There is no room in Olivier's feelgood romantic ending for lines such as these:

King Harry	. . . And you may, some of you, thank love for my blindness, who cannot see many a fair French city for one fair French maid that stands in my way.
King Charles	Yes my lord, you see them perspectively, the cities turned into a maid – for they are all girdled with maiden walls that war hath never entered.
King Henry	Shall Kate be my wife?
King Charles	So please you. (V.ii.313–21)

Olivier's version is in accordance with the dominant Shakespeare critics of the period; he rewrites (or interprets) the play as right-wing propaganda, a reworking which is still prevalent in Shakespeare's place within the English national curriculum. In a pamphlet produced for the government's 'think-tank' , the Centre for Policy Studies, John Marenbon insists upon the teaching of Shakespeare in terms which are peculiarly close to those of Agee, Wilson and Tillyard. Marenbon calls for the need for students to read Shakespeare (along with other pre-twentieth-century canonical writers) in order to preserve our national heritage. In his evangelical final words he recommends that politicians and committees must keep English literature away from the control of teachers. They must be 'distrustful of experts and chaste towards fashion. May God grant them sharpness of mind and firmness of resolve, for in the future of its language there lies the future of a nation!'[17] In rewriting *Henry V,* Olivier has validated the play and created what has become nationalist, 'authentic' Shakespeare.

Yet I may be unjust to Olivier in expanding on the standard view of the play as propaganda. Although certainly some of the cast had seen active service (Esmond Knight – who plays Fluellen – was blinded in the war and had to be guided around the film set), it seems strangely inappropriate that many of the extras on the film were Irish (who were not involved in the war) and, more peculiarly, Americans, many of whom were absent without leave at the time of filming. The inclusion of these Americans, especially (identifiable by the way they wear their helmets cocked to the side), is slightly unsettling. Additionally, the use of film and theatrical space – or 'real' versus fake – calls our attention to the fictionality of the portrait, especially evident in the closing sequence when the 'real' princess dissolves into the grotesquely painted boy actor. We are brought back to earth and reminded that the film was just an ingenious illusion. When sponsored by the Ministry of Information, it is difficult to do anything other than produce the propaganda required – yet a close reading of the film uncovers some possible reservations concerning the film's overtly political mission.

A speech curiously included is that of Burgundy in the final scene of the play. This speech is a plea for peace, not a celebration of the achievement of peace, as is argued by Wilson Knight when he concludes that 'the play ends in concord', 'Burgundy's pastoral lines crown, as with a chaplet of flowers, Shakespeare's historic sequence.'[18] Burgundy's nostalgia for the past in his meditation on the cost of war is visually accompanied by his prolonged gaze out of the window. Olivier presents here, as he does elsewhere in the film, a play within a play. Burgundy, visually recalling the Chorus's transportation through the painted curtain, glances through the Pol de Limbourg landscape which is metamorphosed into a landscape hitherto unfamiliar in the film. Almost imperceptibly we move forward in time – the rural scenes are close to a Constable landscape – and all of a sudden the audience is confronted with two children standing before a gate. The children provide an illustration for Burgundy's lines, 'Even so our houses and ourselves and children / Have lost, or do not learn for want of time, / The sciences that should become our country, / But grow like savages' (V.ii.56–9). This image of the boy and girl by the gate (visually recalling the gates of Harfleur, the gates

Katherine sees opening in the garden as well as the passageways through the painted curtain and painted window)[19] lasts only fleetingly (without a video to rewind and pause it could easily be missed by a cinema audience). These children belong to 1944 rather than 1415 – the image is photographic, the children, barefoot and poor, are superimposed on a still-landscape, evocative of wartime evacuees engaged in a game of make-believe. A close inspection of this sequence reveals that they are filmed rather than photographed: the boy actually blinks. On careful viewing, the audience's point of view has shifted: no longer are we looking *through* the painted window, we are looking *at* the painted window. The camera lifts up from the boy and girl to reveal the painted Louvre, where Burgundy was a few minutes before. Burgundy's voice-over (that of the actor Valentine Dyall) – although mourning the passing of the old world – is blatantly reassuring and slightly patronising in tone. This is one place in the film where the morale-boosting tone of the voice-over, the contents of the speech, and the visuals are strangely at odds. A rare note of censure appears in Harry Geduld's full-length celebration of Olivier's film when he glosses over this sequence:

> Here the visuals supply a superfluous and rather too picturesque objectification of Burgundy's images of neglect, ruin and devastation; they culminate ineffectively in a glimpse of two attractive children leaning over a fence – supposedly representing the savage state to which war reduces children.[20]

Surely, the effect of these children 'representing the savage state to which war reduces children' is unsettling rather than reassuring.

As mentioned earlier, it is well known that Olivier made the film under the auspices of the Ministry of Information and that the film was designed as propaganda, or escapist fantasy which glamorises war and boosts morale. The film is concerned with transportations from one state to another – from theatre to film and from one moment in history to another. The means by which this is achieved are visualised in the image of the Chorus looking through the painted curtain and Burgundy looking through the painted window, intermediaries for the spectator watching the film. It is possible that embedded in the text is a slight note of caution and a potential critique of the escapism offered by the film as a whole. If we go too far beyond the curtain or if we look too closely at the film, we may, like Dorothy when she finally comes face to face with the Wizard of Oz, find ourselves, alarmingly, very much in our own time.

Kenneth Branagh's *Henry V*

In 1989 the play was filmed by Kenneth Branagh, seemingly in an attempt to rescue *Henry V* from its status as propaganda. Dubbed in *The Times* on the day before *Henry V's* release as 'the young pretender', Branagh claimed that the play needed 'to be reclaimed from jingoism and World War Two associations'.[21] Without doubt, Branagh's film both pays homage to its predecessor while seemingly recovering the history for an 1980s audience.

In his production of *Henry V*, Kenneth Branagh reverses many of the editorial decisions of Olivier; most notably, not to appear anti-European, he turns the French into worthy opponents and even makes the Dauphin a likeable figure. As with all film versions of Shakespeare, speeches have to be reduced in order to make the plays filmic – the long speeches freeze the action and can be boring to watch. As in the Olivier version, Branagh's Chorus is fragmented so that a few lines punctuate the action rather than suspend it. On the rare occasions when speech does suspend action, it has a shock effect on the audience. Such is the case of Judi Dench's rendering of Mistress Quickly's account of Falstaff's death and the rebuke to the King by Michael Williams (either deliberately or coincidentally played by the actor, Michael Williams), suggesting that Henry's cause is unjust and his word untrustworthy. Here we have close-ups, concentrating on the suffering of the individual and posing a question mark over the ethical position of the King. Henry himself achieves this intense visual scrutiny in his desperate prayer to the God of Battles on the eve of Agincourt. Initially it would seem that the close-ups are used by Branagh to question rather than approve the King's actions. Certainly, unlike Olivier's production, Branagh's film is – at least, initially – striking for its *inclusions* rather than its exclusions.[22]

Perhaps the most notable of these inclusions are the sentencing of the conspirators and the hanging of Bardolph (which Branagh shows rather than simply reporting). Branagh also includes flashbacks to the *Henry IV* plays, depicting Falstaff and crew in the tavern, ostensibly to suggest Henry's betrayal of his comrades. The flashbacks are used again with the hanging of Bardolph and in the final moments of the film. We begin with Henry as an impenetrable mask of monarchy, presented as ruthless, distrustful and potentially evil. He tricks the conspirators and the atmosphere is one of tension – there are spies everywhere and the King can only maintain his position through subterfuge. The archbishops, unlike the ineffectual jokey figures of Olivier, are conspiring together, hardly holy figures, but shrewd and corrupt politicians. The King enters the film literally cloaked in darkness, forecasting the disguised king on the eve of the Battle of Agincourt. For an 1980s audience, the inhuman, black-masked figure inevitably recalls Darth Vader in *Star Wars* (1977), and thus the audience is invited to regard the King – as does Michael Williams in the later scene – with the utmost suspicion. (Ian McKellen repeats the allusion in the opening sequence of *Richard III*, 1995, the gas-masked invaders combined with the heavy breathing of the disguised Richard recall even more vividly the initial entrance of Darth Vader in *Star Wars*.) As in the Olivier film, Branagh takes the image of doors opening to visually connect different scenes. The dark figure of Henry (seen from behind) framed by a door is used in the publicity posters for the film. Branagh underlines the fact that this is a Henry capable of opening doors, in the Machiavellian sense of using his position of power to seize every opportunity. The doors open for the King at the beginning of the film, and they close on Scroop and his fellow-conspirators in Southampton. While Renee Asherson in Olivier's film is confined within doors and, like a damsel in distress, is liberated from the effete French by the swashbuckling Olivier, Emma Thompson's Katherine opens the door to discover the gloomy and desperate world of her careworn father (played by Paul Scofield, whose French King visually recalls his portrayal in Peter Brook's *Lear*). The opening of doors in the film forecasts and recalls the battering of the gates of Harfleur. The film ends with the doors slamming on the English and French court.

This dark side of Henry is in direct contrast to Olivier's portrayal and is undoubtedly the product of the influential new historicist or cultural materialist revisionist readings of the mid-1980s, most notably Stephen Greenblatt's 'Invisible Bullets' (*Shakespearean Negotiations*, 1988) and Jonathan Dollimore and Alan Sinfield's 'History and Ideology: The Instance of *Henry V*' (in *Alternative*

Shakespeares, ed. John Drakakis, 1985). The picture of Branagh's Henry at the beginning of the film is in keeping with Stephen Greenblatt's account of a Henry who 'deftly registers every nuance of royal hypocrisy, ruthlessness and bad faith – testing, in effect, the proposition that successful rule depends not upon sacredness but upon demonic violence'.[23] Branagh seems to do to Olivier what Dollimore and Sinfield do to E. M. W. Tillyard in attacking the notion of a natural hierarchical order in Shakespeare. Dollimore and Sinfield consider the strategies of power and 'the anxieties informing both them and their ideological representation'.[24] The human cost of imperial ambition is revealed through Henry's own ideological justifications. This is most apparent in the play text in Henry's exchange with Michael Williams, when Henry tries to rid himself of the responsibility of war; although the disguised Henry insists that the King will keep his word he later fails to keep his word to Williams – the glove is returned without the promised fight, subtly confirming Williams's assertion that Henry – because he *is* a king – will not be true to his word. Henry, in the play text, in several respects resembles Machiavelli's ideal prince; and this episode is very close to Machiavelli's chapter on why a prince should [not] keep his word.[25] Fluellen's historicising of Henry's war (the continual comparison of his prince to ancient predecessors is like Machiavelli's own method of analysis) results in an unintentional truth (resembling the Machiavellian advice that a Prince must know his friends well, his enemies better): Fluellen notes that Alexander 'did in his ales and his angers, look you, kill his best friend Cleitus' (IV.vii.36–7). Although the comparison stops here for Gower – 'Our king is not like him in that. He never killed any of his friends' (IV.viii.38–9) – in denying the likeness, he affirms it. Inevitably the comparison recalls Henry's sentencing of Scroop (whom Henry claims, 'knew'st the very bottom of my soul', I.ii.94) and, of course, his former companion, Falstaff (of whom the Hostess observes, the 'king has killed his heart', II.i.84).

The chiaroscuro effects of the dark beginning of Branagh's *Henry V* hark back to Orson Welles's *film noir, Chimes At Midnight* (1967), in which Welles's Falstaff is incrementally reduced and brutalised by a self-aware and self-serving Prince Hal. Branagh's throned Henry visually recalls John Gielgud's cold and isolated Henry IV, the Darth Vader (or dark father) of Welles's film. Through a series of intertextual references – flashbacks to other plays and films – the film initially seems to build a picture of Henry who is hostile and repellent. The close-up and flashback, however, rather than questioning his motives, ultimately soften and humanise the figure. When Bardolph is being hung, Branagh has Henry recall through flashback the ribald days of the tavern, while the close-up reveals his eyes to be moist – the tears blending with the rain. After the prayer to the god of battles in which Henry acknowledges his father's guilt in taking Richard's crown, there are definite tears in the King's eyes, and in his union with Fluellen after victory, he is definitely weeping. The vulnerability of the king in this scene is contrasted with *and* compared to the slaughtered boys. As David Robinson notes on the eve of the film's UK release: 'Branagh's Henry is strictly according to the Geneva Convention.'[26] The image of the King carrying the dead boy – a former companion of his 'wild Hal' days and a victim of his dubious war[27] – provides the emblem of the film, used in much of the publicity pictures: it visualises the ambivalence of this production which simultaneously glorifies and condemns Henry's war. Youth has been sacrificed; the King emerges at the end of the film as a 'real man'.

Branagh's *Henry V* does not inspire feelings of nationalism, as in the Olivier film, but rather, as Graham Holderness remarks, conveys the *emotions of patriotism*.[28] But these emotions grip you unawares. The first third of the film is markedly anti-war and anti-patriotic; but by the end, the audience is cheering the King alongside his rebel ranks (like the opportunistic and corrupt Pistol and Nym, who can't help but feel inspired by the St Crispin's Day speech).

It is often noted that the film, made in the late 1980s, following the lead of Adrian Noble's 1984 production (in which Branagh played the title role), is made as a post-Falklands, anti-war production. The realism of the piece is in direct contrast to the painted scenery of Olivier's version (with the exception of the fanciful scene depicting the English coast behind the Chorus: Derek Jacobi looks as if he's literally standing on a map of Great Britain).[29] Branagh imitates and pays tribute to Olivier, following in his footsteps by commencing his film career, like Olivier's, by directing and starring in *Henry V*, a play which appropriately dramatises a young man's rite of passage. The St Crispin's Day speech offers a clear visual 'flashback' to Olivier – Branagh uses a cart, like Olivier, as a humble platform for his rousing words. Likewise, Branagh imitates or rivals Olivier in the hail of arrows filed in unison by the British foot-soldiers at the beginning of the battle sequence.

The film, however, also pays tribute to contemporary Vietnam War films – or the 'buddy film' – which present a simultaneous fascination and contempt for war.[30] Chris Fitter has argued that through the rhetoric of class transcendence, Branagh's film conveys the double message that war is hell, but it also heroises.[31] Unlike Olivier's *Henry V*, Branagh's film was not paid for by the government but was made in spite of reduced subsidies. Branagh's own company, Renaissance Films plc, shows how success can be achieved, like Henry's war, against all the odds. It gained a BAFTA and Academy Award and made money (approximately £7.5 million). Quick on the heels of the film's critical success, Japan's giant Sony Corporation made an investment in Renaissance Films.[32] Branagh's Henry V, unlike the aristocratic characterisation of Olivier, reveals throughout his working-class Belfast origins; he is the epitome of the self-made man who rises from the common ranks through sheer entrepreneurialism. Branagh himself, in his autobiography, *Beginning*, has underlined the similarities between himself and Shakespeare's King when he first undertook the role at Stratford: 'Henry was a young man, and so was I. He was faced with an enormous responsibility. I didn't have to run the country and invade France, but I did have to control Brian Blessed and open the Stratford season.'[33] During the filming of *Henry V*, Branagh was inevitably prone to making comparisons between his and Henry's predicament. In fact, his diary of the shooting reads like a rewriting of Shakespeare's play, climaxing in Branagh's cutting his Harfleur wall-shaped birthday cake. Branagh's identification is with a king who has more in common with Richard Branson than Winston Churchill – he seems to have grown out of an age of football hooliganism and the conquest of privatisation. He is constructed as Margaret Thatcher's ideal hero. In fact, it has been suggested that during her time as Prime Minister, Mrs Thatcher could be seen herself as auditioning for the title role in her own production of *Henry V*.[34]

Eventually Henry is transformed into the ideal 1980s man: rugged, yet a lover of children, confident yet self-mocking. Clearly, this Henry struck a chord: contemporary reviews are full of praise for the inspirational tone of the production. Kenneth Rothwell begins his review by declaring: 'Kenneth Branagh's *Henry V* is, and will be recognised as, one of the outstanding Shakespeare movies of the century.'[35]

T. O'Brien, writing in *Commonweal*, makes the extraordinary state-ment: 'in some ways (if this be heresy, make the most of it), Branagh improves on Shakespeare'.[36] Allegedly Prince Charles – Patron of Branagh's company – cried. In fact, Branagh's version, although initially questioning Henry's manipulation of power, ultimately confirms his right to rule.

The Chorus – a seemingly inappropriate figure for a film – is retained by Branagh as he was by Olivier, to manipulate our reactions and engage us with the action. In the play text, Shakespeare's Chorus calls attention to the inadequacies of theatre, continually reminding us that we are watching a play. Branagh's Chorus, played by Derek Jacobi, dressed in a modern replica of a World War I trench coat, introduces the play on the film set as if he were the director. His purpose seems to be, therefore, to remind us that we are watching a film. Yet later he is at the edge of the action, commenting in a vein reminiscent of BBC coverage of the Falklands war by reporter Brian Hanrahan, who became increasingly identified with the war he was covering. Initially Jacobi's Chorus seems cynical and detached. As the action develops, his emotional involvement builds – in fact, a careful viewing of his face at the end of the film reveals a wound, as if he has directly participated in the Battle of Agincourt.[37] He literally changes face, and this conversion from cynical observer to enthusiastic recruit mirrors the *volte-face* of the film as a whole.

Harold Innocent's Burgundy suggests a bald-headed, Conservative politician, a cross between Churchill and the soon to be Arts Minister, David Mellor. Visually and verbally he ties all the loose ends together; the flashbacks accompanying his lament for the wastes of war, while concentrating on the victims of Henry's reign, provide the audience with a filmic curtain call, inviting us to savour the glorious moments of the film. Unlike Valentine Dyall's Burgundy, Harold Innocent's Burgundy is ultimately determined to look on the bright side; there is a sense of satisfaction in what has been achieved rather than lost in war. Harry Geduld, in his review of the film, singles out Burgundy's speech as reminding us of Henry's 'gross mistreatment of his former comrades and of the massacre of the camp-boys who had accompa-nied his campaign'.[38] But Burgundy's tone is unmistakably light-hearted; and rather than looking *forward*, this Burgundy looks *backward* – not to the ravages of war (as in the Olivier version) but back to images of merry England. The audience is invited not to mourn, but applaud the jolly faces paraded before us. Similarly, Branagh's film looks backward – while appearing to oppose Olivier's patriotic glorification of war and nationalisation of Shakespeare, it ultimately applauds it, reaffirming the myth of 'authentic Shakespeare'.

Initially, Branagh's film seems to call attention to the play's ironies, seemingly interrogating its own political premises. But, if anything, Branagh's film is more a product of right-wing ideology than is Olivier's; while Olivier daringly pierces the illusion of stability in Burgundy's elegiac speech bringing the film audience into their own time, Branagh takes us back in time, cunningly consolidating Shakespeare as an ideological force: the fighting spirit of the British combined with the immortal lines of Shakespeare provide an ideal British export, a force to be reckoned with abroad. While initially bringing Shakespeare into the late twentieth century, calling into question Henry's imperialistic ambitions, Branagh ultimately takes us back in time, reaffirming the views of Tillyard, Wilson Knight, and perhaps even those responsible for Shakespeare teaching within the English National Curriculum.

As Lesley Aers has argued in 'Shakespeare in the National Curriculum', Shakespeare is seen as a compulsory part of the study of English, culturally important and supplying 'universal values'.[39] Any comparison of Branagh's film with contemporary Shakespeare studies seems to reinforce what Simon Barker has identified as a growing gap between Shakespeare criticism and the ways in which Shakespeare is taught in British schools.[40] There is an equivalent gap, I would suggest, between Shakespeare criticism and the ways in which Shakespeare is projected on screen. Branagh's film thereby joins in a 'holy war', not with the government (and 'jingoistic' Shakespeare), but with academics long fed up with such bardolatry. As Richard Wilson has noted, the evacuation of historical content from the plays and the evangelical belief in the 'universality' of Shakespeare is evident in Rex Gibson's Shakespeare and Schools Project.[41] The Cambridge School Shakespeare texts, unashamedly, invite us to ignore what has gone before; according to the preface to *The Taming of the Shrew,* for example, 'you are encouraged to make up your own mind . . . rather than having someone else's interpretation handed down to you'.[42] The purpose of these 'user-friendly' texts – full of 'fun' exercises and easy explanations – is ultimately to 'convert' us to the view that Shakespeare is timeless and to keep us away from dangerous critics who may suggest otherwise. Yet, as John Drakakis reminds us, this 'universality' is essentially 'English'; Shakespeare's presence in the media is normally hidden in quotations (such as the headline breaking the news of Princess Diana's death, 'Goodnight sweet Princess'),[43] quotations which are a 'manifestation of Shakespearean "presence", whatever the context', signifying that which 'is essentially the model of 'Englishness''.[44]

To return to Branagh's film, it could be said that it is designed with an eye to providing a marketable teaching resource, a teaching resource which inspires national pride in an appreciation (rather than understanding) of Shakespeare. Branagh's mission is to convert us first to Henry and then to Shakespeare. The religious atmosphere of the end of the film, reinforced by the City of Birmingham Symphony Orchestra's *Non nobis domine* ('Not unto us, O Lord, not unto us, but unto thy name give glory') is a point which is hard to miss. The music, which begins with the mournful tones of a solo singer and ends with a rousing chorus and orchestra (similar in effect to *Land of Hope and Glory*), combines the forces of spiritual celebration and national anthem, paying tribute to Shakespeare's (and Branagh's) achievement. Wilson Knight's words are worth quoting again here as they are, surprisingly, more akin to the ultimate message of Kenneth Branagh in 1989 than of Laurence Olivier in 1945: 'we need expect no Messiah, but we might, at this hour, turn to Shakespeare'.[45]

Branagh's *Henry V* is a Hollywood-styled, consumer-driven production in the tradition of *Star Wars*; while seeming to speak for future generations, it is a flashback, a tale of long ago. Henry begins the film as Darth Vader and is gradually transformed into Luke Skywalker – or Ben (Obi Wan) Kenobi (visually suggested when the King visits the battle camp in disguise). And, like *Star Wars*, this nationalistic 'authentic' Shakespeare belongs to a world of make-believe.

6 Conclusions

This book has privileged 'issues' over film texts or directors, refusing to regard the latter two as precious objects to be valued in their own right. Rather a film text or the work of 'auteurs' of Shakespeare, directors with recognisable styles, such as Olivier, Zeffirelli, or Branagh, have to be seen as readings/receptions and to be taken together rather than individually. Only in this way can we uncover what insights and/or crimes are committed in the name of Shakespeare.

As previously contended,[1] Shakespeare on film is attractive to the market as a means of gaining a special kind of 'cultural capital'; there is a belief that Shakespeare contains positive values transmitted through an unparalleled form of entertainment. Rather than 'for all time', this book regards Shakespeare films to be 'of an age' while interrogating the myth that no matter how diluted the movie version of the play might be, it is thought that experience of Shakespeare on film can in some ways instruct better or convert the viewer. I have considered the ways in which films of Shakespeare's plays, like literary criticism, produce different views on issues such as violence (by, to a greater extent, pretending it is absent from Shakespeare's plays); gender (film changes gender roles, producing different Ophelias and Gertrudes according to contemporary attitudes towards women); sexuality (the films examined here, against the evidence, promote different models of 'wholesome' heterosexuality); race (films either obliterate race or racialism in order to preserve an image of a 'white' Shakespeare or highlight race by using black actors, presumably to argue for Shakespeare as a Renaissance racial campaigner, a mission doomed to failure); and finally, nationalism (Shakespeare's plays are manipulated for propagandistic purposes, reconfigured to celebrate 'this England' as some kind of 'other Eden' or 'demi-paradise').

The representation of nationalism is perhaps a key to the success of

Shakespeare on screen: there is a belief that the words of Shakespeare contain some sort of 'magic' and this is a magic which is peculiar to English. This 'Englishness', while in the UK referring to place, is appropriated by Americans to embrace the English language itself, asserting a chauvinistic view of the rightful pre-eminence of English as *the* spoken language. Even Baz Luhrmann, whose *Romeo + Juliet* makes minimum use of the play text, undaunted by claims that Shakespeare belongs to the UK, confidently proclaimed a commonly held view among academics in the United States and Canada: 'Shakespeare wrote basically for an American accent.'[2]

I have suggested elsewhere that Franco Zeffirelli's films of Shakespeare (and possibly non English-speaking, cartoon and silent film adaptations)[3] covertly and daringly imply that pictures can speak as loudly and eloquently as words – even *Shakespeare's* words. These adaptations, on one level, set themselves up as competitors in terms of genre (film versus literature) or nationality (Italianness versus Englishness, for example). Film, after all, is not a linguistic medium; words are sacrificed to visual effects. However, in English-speaking adaptations, a certain reverence for the text or the words is usually the case. Rather than arrogance, humility is expected. In fact, one of the original reasons for filming Shakespeare is, perhaps, still present today.

Shakespeare on screen began in the early twentieth century as filmed theatre, as in the Gaumont–Hepworth *Hamlet* of 1913. This film's aim was to record the famous performance of Forbes-Robertson as a memento for those fortunate enough to see him in the role and as a substitute for those who hadn't experienced 'the real thing'.[4] The acknowledgement of films of Shakespeare as derivative or inferior to 'the real thing' persists. For instance, Peter Greenaway has Caliban scoop Shakespeare's plays out of the water in the concluding moments of his film; initially seen urinating and defecating on Prospero's books, Caliban, like Greenaway himself, although a dese-crater of books, nonetheless preserves Shakespeare for future genera-tions.[5] The *Folio* (identifiable from the initials W. S. and the Droeshout portrait) is glimpsed briefly in the final moments of the film; as Douglas Lanier has noted, Prospero's hand points to Jonson's prefatory poem which asks the reader to 'looke/Not on his Picture, but his Booke'.[6] Greenaway's point that we should 'looke/Not on his Picture, but his Booke', that an adapter is necessarily a desecrater of

Shakespeare is, undoubtedly, a commonly held belief – and one which seems to be built into 'successful' English-speaking film adaptations of Shakespeare. This, it seems, is what is meant by 'faithful' to Shakespeare; and what the fidelity debate is all about. Witness, for example, the final moments of Kenneth Branagh's *Hamlet*. The glittering aristocratic beauty of the Danish court is juxtaposed with the grey uniformed soldiers of Fortinbras's army who are seen, at the close of the film, destroying the monument to King Hamlet in an act of supreme disrespect. (After a close visual scrutiny, I am certain that the statue is actually crying.) A new age (one of dull mechanical reproduction?) takes over from the old; the implication is, perhaps, that the film simultaneously destroys and preserves *Hamlet*.

Although this book, for the most part, has restricted itself to 'straight' film adaptations of Shakespeare, I will end with a brief evaluation of three films which just sneak into the Shakespeare-on-screen canon – examples of what I have called 'conversion to Shakespeare narratives' – Kenneth Branagh's *In the Bleak Midwinter* (1995), Al Pacino's *Looking for Richard* (1996) and (briefly) John Madden's *Shakespeare in Love* (1998). These films have been chosen because they are adaptations concerned with the process of adaptation itself, deriving from the musical 'let's put on a show' genre. They provide us with a filmic explanation of the underlying processes and purposes of filming Shakespeare.

The British title of Branagh's film, *In the Bleak Midwinter*, is most familiar to us from the Christmas carol in which a speaker, overwhelmed by his inferiority, ultimately learns that he can give something to the Christ child: 'What shall I give Him? Give Him my heart.'[7] The American title, *A Midwinter's Tale*, calls attention both to its Christmas setting and its Shakespearean theme; but the carol is still prominent – played on the soundtrack on an acoustic guitar – in the most poignant moments of the film and in the final credits. Certainly, the story of a director/actor's 'need' to produce *Hamlet* during the Christmas season in an abandoned church in a village called 'Hope' reinforces an Arnoldian belief that Shakespeare should be brought to the masses, that 'great literature' can improve our lives. In the film, Shakespeare's name becomes virtually synonymous with 'hope'. The church setting is, in this sense, the ideal set for *Hamlet*; while the director/actor, played by Michael Maloney, is mockingly referred to as 'Sir Laurence', the film also pays homage to Olivier's *Hamlet* in its church-like interior and its mission to 'convert' the performers and the audience to Shakespeare. Branagh virtually rewrites *Hamlet* as *A Christmas Carol*; as a result of a 'visitation' by Shakespeare, everyone's lives are improved, both spiritually and financially.

Al Pacino's film, similarly, draws parallels between actors and characters, focusing on the American contribution to Shakespeare studies. British actors such as John Gielgud, Derek Jacobi and Kenneth Branagh, as well as 'scholars', in interview, comment on the play but it is ultimately up to Al Pacino and his sidekick, Frederic Kimball, to make up their minds about how to produce/perform the play and to shake off their sense of inferiority as Americans. Their mission is to make Shakespeare more accessible, revealing the 'feeling' behind his words; and interviews with ordinary people are juxtaposed with rehearsals and final performances. After an exhausting death scene, Pacino, playing Richard, clearly looks as though he has discovered something; but the feeling of enormous reward is undermined by the figure of Shakespeare, sitting alone in the audience, silently shaking his head.

Finally, the most daring of the 'let's put on a Shakespeare play' film is, of course, *Shakespeare in Love*, in which we have the dramatist himself in the throes of passion and creation. The focus on the audience's silent amazement after the final moments of *Romeo and Juliet* acts as an intermediary between the filmed play and the film audience; by implication, we also have been 'transformed' by the experience. As a caption in the *Guardian* put it: '*Shakespeare in Love* . . . is bringing the Bard new audiences.'[8]

Perhaps it is time to rethink the way we interpret Shakespeare on film; film adaptations do not have to be simply regarded as pale versions of 'the real thing' which, nonetheless, are of unique value insofar as they bring us closer to the 'greatness' which is Shakespeare. In 1985, Graham Holderness suggested in an influential and groundbreaking essay on the use of films within the English curriculum that there are essentially two types of Shakespeare films, those which 'operate simply as vehicles for the transmissions of ideology' and those which 'block, deflect or otherwise 'work on' ideology in order partially to disclose its mechanisms'.[9] Holderness gives examples of the first type in (most of) the BBC Time-Life televised Shakespeare (1975–85) and the second type in Akira Kurosawa's *Throne of Blood* (1957). Sadly, it is normally the former type which educational institutions both utilise and scorn. Holderness quotes despairing school examiners, among them the following lament:

> . . . most candidates appeared to know *Macbeth* well. Some, however, were handicapped by having seen a film version . . . candidates should remember that it is Shakespeare's text which is being examined.[10]

In other words, films of Shakespeare threaten to produce students such as Cher in *Clueless*, who may not know her *Hamlet* but does indeed know her Mel Gibson. Instead of taking the view that films 'subvert' traditional approaches to Shakespeare (in the example quoted, students subvert traditional approaches by privileging the film over the play text), Holderness argues that most screen versions of Shakespeare seek to uphold the status quo. The conservative values which Holderness sees embedded in these films, I would argue, are encapsulated in a reverence for Shakespeare, what Holderness later describes as 'bardolatry'.[11]

Returning to *Clueless*, it might be more fruitful to consider the likes of Cher not as the product of an illiterate age, but rather, a post-literate age in which the visual image dominates. Rather than using film to 'understand' or 'get closer' to Shakespeare, this book has concentrated on the power of the visual image and the ways in which Shakespeare is manipulated on screen to perpetuate different views on violence, gender, sexuality, race and nationalism. It is the name 'Shakespeare' which, dangerously, sanctifies the presentation of the issues. Above all, the study of Shakespeare on screen should interrogate what is behind the name, challenging the assumption that if it is Shakespeare, it must be right. As it is pointed out in the film, *Shakespeare in Love*, 'he's only the author'.

Appendix I: Student Exercises

What follows are examples of student work. Examine the excerpts and evaluate: argument, fluency, depth and/or breadth of reading, and evidence of independent thinking. Finally, and most importantly, identify the strengths of the work and how a particular approach illuminates an understanding of the play. Once you have reached your decision, turn to Appendix 2 and see if our evaluations agree. The aims and objectives of each of the following assignments are:

1. To read canonical texts in non-canonical ways, thereby exposing readings as constructed.
2. To examine how film can serve as a critical tool for interpreting – or reinterpreting – Shakespeare.
3. To analyse the interplay between text and image.

1. **Choose a critical book or essay on one of Shakespeare's plays and compare it to a scene/sequence from the same play on screen (produced in the same period, that is, within six years). Discuss the ideological assumptions underlying the critics' account and the director's version of the play.**

(i) Romeo and Juliet

The sixties was a period where youth culture dominated not only the political scene, but also the literary and artistic spheres. The critics of the sixties consequently began recognising and exploring the pro-youthism aspects of *Romeo and Juliet*. Likewise directors such as Zeffirelli fully exploited these aspects. Zeffirelli began the decade with the first pro-youthism stage version of the play (preceded in approach only by Renato Castelani's 1954 film). It was a revolutionary interpretation of *Romeo and Juliet*. The play had previously been portrayed as being formal, idealistic and romantic. Zeffirelli found the dynamic, realistic interpretation, focusing on the young characters and ridiculing the old. His film, eight years later, incorporated much the same angle. It was released the same year that Nicholas Brooke's book *Shakespeare's Early Tragedies*, including an essay on *Romeo and Juliet*, was published. Although Brooke does not directly discuss the youthism aspects of the play, he does raise concerns that align with the emphasis accentuated by Zeffirelli. He is primarily concerned with the surface and hidden levels of the play and discusses them in terms of structure and language.

Arguably the most important scene in the play and certainly the turning point of the action and tone, is Act 3, scene 1. The death of Mercutio causes Romeo to have a dramatic change of character in seeking his revenge, revealing the 'serpent heart hid with a flow'ring face!' (III.ii.73). Brooke describes it as a scene of 'double climax'; the high point of both the private alliance between Romeo and Juliet and the public battle between the Montagues and Capulets. The scene incorporates both the interior and exterior sides of the plot and therefore encompasses all the major elements in the play. Gaston Bachelard's exploration into 'the dialectics of outside and inside'[1] can be applied to the film version of this scene in terms of *mise en scène:*

> The cinema has the capacity to juxtapose inside and outside worlds and create visual images of opposition.[2]

Romeo and Juliet is about opposites (and as Brooke discusses, the close proximity of those opposites) and this was another area of interest for the critics at the time of Zeffirelli's film. Spencer opens his introduction to the 1967 Penguin edition with a listing of the paradoxical elements within the play.[3] Zeffirelli captures the extent of these disparate forces by manipulating the structure, language and visual motifs. Brooke's discussion of the play is largely preoccupied with the play's formal structure and how it is emphasised, but also questioned. He explores the 'inner experience' beneath the 'formal surface'[4] which was the essence of Zeffirelli's film; the realistic elements beneath the idealism. Brooke compares *Romeo and Juliet* to a 'stately dance'.[5] He recognises the formality of structure, language and images presented in the play.

. . .

It can be concluded therefore that what both Brooke and Zeffirelli were searching for was the reality amidst the artificiality. They recognised the formal structure of events and language, but beneath them found a fresh approach, a realistic solidity holding the play together. Brooke described what he felt was real could be 'perceived between the opposite polarities of ceremony and unceremoniousness'.[6] Zeffirelli developed those areas to such an extent that even the moments of ceremony in his film seem vitally real. Both these interpreters can be seen to have a sixties' attitude towards a play, that seems to belong to that decade. The critic questions formality and intellectual language. The director fills his frame with action, life and characters that appeal to the contemporary young audience. Indeed the film has been labelled a 'youth movie',[7] that glorifies and celebrates the young. Brooke and Zeffirelli's approach was much more than this. They revealed a politically significant understanding of *Romeo and Juliet.*

Both Brooke and Zeffirelli recognised the spirit and passion in Shakespeare's words, particularly in the duel scene. They saw its potential to be portrayed as a realistic demonstration of revelry, masculine pride, friendship and intense love and hate. They understood its intellectual 'inferiority', but also its spiritual 'superiority' to the world of the common day.[8]

(ii) Much Ado About Nothing

Jean E. Howard, in her essay 'Renaissance antitheatricality and the politics of gender and rank in *Much Ado About Nothing'* (in *Shakespeare Reproduced: The Text in History and Ideology,* ed. Jean E. Howard and M. O'Connor, London: Methuen, 1987), suggests a more definite ideological meaning within the play. She sees a struggle between those who have power within a community and those who wrongly aspire to this power. She stresses a class struggle, hence her use of 'politics' within her title. This suggests a possible negotiation of rank within a class culture, as well as identifying a constant gender conflict. The latter is perhaps more a struggle over identity, rather than over power and leadership within society.

By comparing sequences from the Branagh screen version of the play with Howard's essay I shall consider what ideologies both the director and critic identify within the text and how they see these as manifesting themselves. I shall also consider how the differing roles of director versus critic affect their interpretations of *Much Ado About Nothing*. This may lead them to take different ideologies for granted when realising their aims either on screen or on paper.

. . .

This delay before allowing Leonato to speak not only gives Branagh the opportunity to stress the community over the individual, but also introduces Beatrice as his main character. She speaks the words of a song not intended for a female, let alone the 'wittiest' *(Independent, 27.8.93)* and strongest of Shakespeare's female characters. He seems to be stressing the ideology of the female within this particular community. This seems to gain further importance when Leonato speaks directly to Hero about Claudio's 'honour' (I.i.10), blatantly referring to an affection on her part for him which is not within the original text. This is followed by Beatrice's witticisms about Benedick. She wins this 'merry war' (I.i.57) with the Messenger on this occasion, by 'stopping his mouth' with a grape!

Howard agrees that gender is an issue within this play. However, as Branagh seems to celebrate the strength of women, Howard sees the text reinforcing women's subordination to men, their weakness within society, and their punishment for transgressing accepted gender boundaries.

. . .

Both director and critic work within the ideological institutions of the theatre, cinema, literature and academia. Each discipline has its own associated ideologies which may impose restraints, in that ideologies may serve to promote conformity to societies' norms and expectations. However, does the cinema work within a modern ideology of entertainment, which subverts the elitism of literature and undermines the ideology of learning within academia?

By comparing the Branagh version of *Much Ado About Nothing* with Howard's essay on the same, it does seem that there are ideological similarities but with interpretative differences. Both stress the central notion of the community within the play, yet Branagh seeks an egalitarian, non-gendered, non-racist utopia, whereas Howard can only see a society with inevitable class, gender and race divides.

Branagh may be trying to mediate with society by using the medium of film to promote an optimistic view that synthesises the individual's identity along with the benefits of a sharing community. Perhaps this is less realistic than Howard's view of trying to survive within a community despite its contradicting ideologies. Nevertheless, by combining film with literature and synthesising their different ideological interpretations, a wider range of meaning may be gained through this relationship.

2. Compare and contrast representations of sexuality in one play by Shakespeare with a film/televisual adaptation of the same text.

(i) Much Ado About Nothing

Since its release in 1993, Kenneth Branagh's film version of *Much Ado About Nothing* has once again raised awareness of the accessibility of Shakespeare's plays. *Much Ado About Nothing* is a multi-faceted play presented in the form of a comedy of wits and love. Branagh himself has described it as a play about ' . . . the power of lust; our obsession with sex and the flesh'[9] which goes only part of the way to relating the concern with sexuality of both Shakespeare's play and also Branagh's film version. Shakespeare creates a stage in which the boundaries of masculinity and femininity are categorically defined through the histories of male and female characters, their speeches, and in certain cases (Beatrice's in particular) the dissatisfaction with these gender roles, and Branagh presents these perspectives adding a certain amount of three-dimensionality, converting the words from the page to the screen.

From the opening lines of the film, Branagh takes Shakespeare's words and orders them in such a way as to give the semblance of an up-to-date version of the play. In moving the song, 'Sigh no more, ladies . . . ' from Act 2, scene 3, to the opening of the film, recited as poetry by Emma Thompson, Branagh prepares the audience for the battle of the sexes which they are about to witness in the war of wits between Beatrice and Benedick, and the more general battle of women against the deceptions of men represented by the false accusation of Hero. It also suggests a politically correct approach to the rights of women set in this ambiguous period of time, but falls foul of the original text, which denies the female characters speech after their consent to marry which is seen as submission. Beatrice's mouth is stopped both physically and for the remainder of the play after Benedick's dominating action at the end of Act 5, scene 4:

Benedick (*kissing her*) Peace, I will stop your mouth (V.iv.97)

The act of kissing (universally considered a sensual and sexual experience when exchanged between two lovers) is always articulated in *Much Ado About Nothing* as a command or intention to stop a character's mouth (II.i.291–2), which is a preventative method rather than a loving embrace, replacing the words of a female character, once again implying the submission of women and the dominant nature of man.

. . .

There is a sexual injustice in *Much Ado About Nothing* which has lasted through the centuries and is as prominent in contemporary sexual relations as it is in the play – one law for the boys and another for the girls. Benedick is celebrated as a ladies' man, he himself boasts of his popularity ' . . . it is certain I am loved of all ladies' (I.i.118–19) but his sexual appetite, although joked of, disguises a heart which seems disposed to misogyny. Our first intelligence of him implies an adulterous and sexually rampant nature:

Don Pedro	I think this is your daughter.
Leonato	Her mother hath many times told me so.
Benedick	Were you in doubt, sir, that you asked her?
Leonato	Signor Benedick, no; for then were you a child.

(I.i.98–102)

This sexual inconstancy is applauded and congratulated by other men, but for Benedick to have gained such a reputation, the reputations of countless 'maids' must have been sullied, and their virtue is impossible to replace. As Fanny Burney illustrated centuries later, 'nothing is so delicate as the reputation of a woman: it is, at once, the most beautiful and brittle of all human things'.[10] The virginal status of a woman was purely for the satisfaction of her prospective husband so that he could be secure in the knowledge that he was receiving unsoiled goods, so while the men could 'sow their wild oats' and be as free and reckless as they pleased, the women had to exercise supreme self-control or resign themselves to a life of disrepute. It seems that there is a double standard even within the sexuality of women in *Much Ado About Nothing*. If we are to judge by Margaret's behaviour, women of the lower/servant classes may indulge in sexual liaison as their prospects are unpromising, but for a woman of the higher classes such as Hero to be involved in a sexual relationship, or even accused, is enough to ruin her reputation. Sex for Hero's class is considered a sin:

> *Hero*   If I know more of any man alive
>   Than that which maiden modesty doth warrant,
>   Let all my sins lack mercy. (IV.i.180–2)

In Branagh's *Much Ado*, Margaret and Ursula are both targets of lustful designs at the welcoming celebrations in which Beatrice and Hero (representative of the higher classes) prefer intellectual conversations about men rather than the physical experience, implying that they exist on a higher moral plane. Although Margaret is unaware of what she is doing when she is seen at the balcony with Borachio, upon discovery of the deception she does nothing to rectify the situation, and yet Borachio still describes her as 'just and virtuous' (V.i. 294). She is truly a bawdy Shakespearean character, but Branagh obviously considered there to be a sexual boundary between tasteful and distasteful for the cinemagoing audience as he has removed the beginning of Act 5, Scene 2, which contains numerous sexual innuendoes bordering on crudity.

. . .

The sexuality bursts out of both Shakespeare's play and Branagh's film of *Much Ado About Nothing*. Branagh presents the audience with the sexuality of women in low-cut, virginal white dresses and heaving chests, the sexuality of Hollywood stars in leather trousers, the sexuality of bondage and phallic symbols in the scenes in the prison and the sexuality of the homoerotic. Peter Holland has described Kenneth Branagh's *Much Ado* as 'banal populism',[11] which is just the sort of elitist comment which has prevented the progression of Shakespeare from an exclusive form of entertainment to a widely accessible, thoroughly enjoyable experience of a sexually potent romp, for so many years.

(ii) Henry V

. . .

Henry V as directed by Branagh carries all of the hallmarks of a glorified war movie. It perpetuates strong images of the Vietnam genre, that of camaraderie in the face of adversity. Cynthia Fuchs defines this as the 'Buddy Politic':

> The buddy movie typically collapses intramasculine differences by effecting an uncomfortable sameness, a transgression of boundaries between self and other, inside and outside, legitimate and illicit.[12]

The social context of such films moves between homosexuality and homophobia and this can be clearly recognised in Shakespeare, in particular where the men are unusually tactile by our twentieth-century standards. Cynthia Fuchs goes on to argue that 'these movies conclude with the partners triumphantly detonating all villains'.[13] This is certainly true in *Henry V* where images of violence between men are highly erotic. To kill is the ultimate climax, an agonising and thrilling release of effort and struggle achieved by the victor of the ultimate sacrifice of the other.

The physical battles between men are highly voyeuristic and loaded with phallic symbolism. At the gates of Harfleur with victory imminent, Henry is pictured on a rampant white horse, with his sword aloft. The sword is directly phallic and when erect in mid-air, its sexual connotation is scarcely disguised. The horse's white colour in this instance is symbolic of Henry's 'just' cause, its rampancy a reflection of the young king's virility. The explosions in the background are climactic and reminiscent of the triumphant detonations identified . . . as a hallmark of 'buddy' films. They add to and fuel the frenzy of the King and his men as they go 'Once more unto the breach dear friends; once more'.

At the Battle of Agincourt, the images become more diverse and complex. The sight and sound of the shooting of the arrows powerfully symbolises ejaculation. Lined up shoulder to shoulder with their weapons, the men achieve simultaneous climax repeatedly. All around is a myriad of sexually charged images: sweating, rearing horses, swords penetrating men's flesh, falling with a splash into a wet and soft field. Is this a connotation of female genitalia? The men are returning to 'Mother Earth'. Pictures of men impaled on wooden stakes suggest penetration, proof of the victor's power over his victim and the ultimate display of virility. As the battle draws to an end, Branagh draws the viewer into a slow motion close-up of the king staggering through the mire, struggling to stay on his feet, with the maximum of stamina. As he flails out with his sword his face contorts and we see nothing besides his agonised facial features. This is the moment of climax and we become the lover who shares it. The male protagonist becomes the object of desire, a spectacle of masculinity. We identify masculinity with action, thought and deed, in contrast to the relatively inanimate attractions of femininity, such as appearance and purity.

3. Compare and contrast representations of nationality in a play text and film/televisual text(s) of the same play.

Henry V

Shakespeare has long been regarded as the property of the English nation, being part of its national culture – 'Shakespeare's is by now a name which evokes reverence'[14] – and is clearly linked to the notion of the great arts. In this way, Shakespeare forms part of England's cultural canon, becoming enmeshed within the emotional response to preserve our 'national heritage'. On the other hand, culture can be defined as 'a signifying system through which . . . a social order is communicated, reproduced, experienced and explored'.[15] This suggests that Shakespeare, as part of our culture, can also be used as a 'national symbol',[16] to engender and encourage the correct establishment response.

Both Laurence Olivier and Kenneth Branagh have reproduced Shakespeare's *Henry V* through the medium of film. However, some forty years separates each version. How has the translation from text to screen affected the production and interpretation of the play? Both Olivier and Branagh directed as well as starred in their own versions. John Collick states that there may be little difference between directing a film and reading a text.[17] ...

...

Branagh's battle, then, stresses the pain of the individual rather than a national victory. However, rather than being 'anti-war', this playing with the emotions seems to glorify the personal redemption gained through war.[18] Was Olivier justified, then, in cutting speeches which may have cast Henry in a negative light, for example the traitors' as well as Bardolph's execution, along with the threats before Harfleur? Jorgens sees these as deliberate 'cuts' to 'heighten the polarity of the English and French'.[19] Branagh, by adding the Falstaff flashbacks from *1* and *2 Henry IV* and Bardolph's execution, as well as retaining the traitor's plot and stressing Henry's relationship with Scroop, ' . . . but the man that was his bedfellow' (II.ii.8), heightens the isolation and personal cost to the King. Similarly, by excluding the female Queen Isabel from his version, Branagh celebrates the masculine teamwork of war. In this way, both directors seem to have appropriated Shakespeare for their own ends.

Davies asserts that both 'films deal essentially with the transformation of history into myth and legend'.[20] Despite these versions being produced in different cultures, by different directors, when viewed now they do seem similar in their nationalistic aims. Both Olivier and Branagh have selected a specific point of view perhaps to manipulate the required response. Both versions may stress a national identity in a period of crisis, thus using 'national history as visionary national unity'.[21] Unity may have been the ultimate aim, but are the projects more self-centred than this? Perhaps we are meant to celebrate the achievements of two personalities, who become successful outside their recognised fields? It seems that by choosing a universal and popular medium to recycle this 'bastion of English culture',[22] both Olivier and Branagh promote their own status within the realms of drama, literature and cinema. But by serving their country in this way they also become national icons.

4. Compare two or more screen versions of a scene. You may consider the relevance of editing, casting, *mise en scène*, etc.

Henry V

. . .

Before the battle commences, Henry gives the famous Feast of Crispin speech. As a rousing battle cry both features had to take into account the climax. On the stage it merely meant the growing audibility of Henry; on the screen, however, the additional use of editing and non-diegetic sound meant that the audience could be manipulated into a fervour for the coming battle. Olivier took great care to render visually the rising excitement, the growing heroism, Henry's persuasiveness and skill in whipping up emotion. With careful use of editing, Henry's hypnotic pull is shown by the slowly gathering soldiers around him. He begins by stroking his white horse, immediately showing Henry's natural heroism. The camera tracks before him, almost as if Henry's own might is driving the camera back. His voice grows in amplitude as he asks his loyal soldiers to follow him, 'For he today that sheds his blood with me,/ Shall be my brother' (IV.iii.61–2). The final touch is Henry atop a cart, above the crowds, a king above mere mortal man, but being able to lift his subjects' spirits. At the point of climax the camera pulls away in a slow movement that conveys all the contagious excitement in his men, with the King shown clearly in relation to them. The scene ends with Harry surrounded by his cheering soldiers. Olivier's use of the camera pull-back shows his unique directing ability. In Hollywood, traditionally, the climax scene is portrayed with a close-up of the face, thereby restricting the range. However, Olivier noted the difference between a screen climax and the Shakespearean climax of a final gesture and loud declamation. So it is that the camera retreats as Henry raises his voice. This is a camera device that Olivier employs at both the defeat of Harfleur and before his landing in France.

Branagh's Feast of Crispin speech is similar to Olivier's, both ending in the same vein. However, due to the 'reality' of Branagh's setting, in muddy woodland, it takes on a less theatrical cry, instead acting as an apology for bringing his people into a battle that they were likely to lose. Using a different stress on the line 'We few, we happy few, we band of brothers' (IV.iii.60), Branagh portrays his

Henry as sympathetic to the coming battle and torment his men will face. His soldiers, rather than looking up with admiration, look instead with gritty reality, knowing the problems they face. However, he too must whip up support for the coming battle, and so surrounded by his servants, and employing a simple cut rather than a pull-back, we can view the growing crowd cheering. The way in which both Henrys react to the coming battle can be seen in the final arrival of the French herald. Branagh asks with desperate anger as to why the messenger 'should . . . mock poor fellow thus?' (IV.iii.93). He realises the awful odds they face. Olivier answers with almost mock humour, and as he sends the herald away they both depart with a wry smile, as if already knowing the outcome of the battle.

Finally the battle commences. The reconstruction of Agincourt in Olivier's version was modelled on Eisenstein's sequence of the battle in *Alexander Nevsky* (1938). He makes full use of colour and editing, underpinned with the musical score by Walton, which helps to give the film a sustained power of movement. Olivier shows the French as deluded fools, they are portrayed as snobbish, waited upon, and isolated from their foot soldiers. War, to them, is a mere game, shown as they toast their expected victory. The only decent character is the French herald, who is far braver than the French King and far nobler than the Dauphin. Branagh represents the French as British equals, a force to be reckoned with. The audience believes Salisbury in the Branagh version when he mutters, 'God's arm strike with us! 'Tis a fearful odds'(*Henry V*, IV.iii.5).

The famous view of the charging French cavalry in Olivier's film, consisting of one long tracking shot, helps to give the audience a sense of the coming participation of battle. The same charge is not seen in Branagh's version – instead the charge is heard and the audience views the British troops' faces – faces that help to give the same feeling of participation of war. It is understandable why Branagh did this. The cavalry charge is one of the most memorable aspects of Olivier's film. Branagh wished to comment on Olivier's version through his own movie, but did not wish to copy it. Instead he inverts the charge scene. Olivier showed the exhilaration and medieval fantasy of the French attack, viewed in all its colour and splendour. Branagh shows the outcome of the charge. Branagh does incorporate a tracking shot but saves it for the end of the battle. The camera moves across the battlefield, across the mutilated corpses and injured

survivors as Henry carries a boy's body in his arms. This is a clear definition of the film's central attack on the values of war, a recognition of
the cost of battle. Where Olivier shows the battle as glorified, Branagh
shows the reality. As Olivier's knights charge from the right to left on
screen, Branagh walks to the right. The inversion is complete.

. . .

**5. Find a scene omitted from a film version(s) of a play and explain
why it has been left out (for example, the boy's soliloquy in *Henry V*).**

Roman Polanski's Macbeth

. . .

In IV.iii, Malcolm tests the loyalty of Macduff by confessing to him
that he, like Macbeth, had been imbued with feelings of treachery,
greed and lust:

> It is myself I mean, in whom I know
> All the particulars of vice so grafted
> That when they shall be opened black Macbeth
> Will seem as pure as snow . . . (IV.iii.51–4)

In Shakespeare's *Macbeth*, Macduff basically assures Malcolm that
Macbeth is the evil one and that Malcolm's thoughts are simply that
and nothing more. However, it can be argued that Polanski has
decided to cut out this scene, so as to give Malcolm's character less
depth and exposure. Polanski does not want the audience to witness
Malcolm's articulate feelings. In a story of an evil and ambitious
society, Malcolm is simply shallow, weak and lazy – topped off with
evil, and through the movie one interprets this. For one is only
allowed to see a certain amount of Malcolm's personality. First, one
witnesses how effortlessly Malcolm becomes 'Prince of Cumberland'.
Second, Malcolm is somewhat disturbed by the Thane of Cawdor's
sardonic farewell, 'long live the king'. Here, Malcolm cannot compre-
hend the man's boldness and strength of conviction in death. Perhaps
in the same situation, Malcolm would have confessed his treasons to
the king, asking pardon. And third, Malcolm flees to England after the
discovery of Duncan's body. This surely sets him up as a somewhat
cowardly man, unable to protect himself.

Polanski conveys further weakness (through omitting a significant part of IV.iii) by having Malcolm earlier offer Macbeth a drink during Macbeth's anxiety over his decision to kill the King. Moreover, at the crucial moment when Macbeth informs his wife that they will 'proceed no further in this business', it is the character of Malcolm that persuades Macbeth to go through with the assassination. For Malcolm smugly hails Macbeth 'Thane of Cawdor'. Perhaps it can be argued that Malcolm also wishes Duncan dead. However, lacking the necessary strength to kill him, he uses irritation to prompt Macbeth.

Ultimately, Polanski, through such omissions of text, has aligned Malcolm with his conception of the play. If society is violent and human nature is naturally corrupt then the individuals who admit it and have the strength to pursue it, deserve respect. Moreover, if Malcolm, Donalbain and Banquo are as evil and ambitious as Macbeth but lack the strength to live it out then surely Macbeth is the character most worthy of respect. At least his evil is honest and open! Reiterating this, Jack Jorgens suggests that Polanski stresses the point that Macbeth displays the courage which is lacking in both Duncan and his sons.[23]

It would appear that Roman Polanski feels strongly that *Macbeth* genuinely mirrors contemporary society. Polanski believes that his exploitation of carnage and bloodbath is directly influenced by our society. This is not surprising when comprehending the fact that his own history is plagued with the horrific murders of his wife and child at the hands of Charles Manson. Indeed there are images in this film that seem to reflect upon the murders. For example, one of Macbeth's visions is a baby sliced out of its mother's body – a direct parallel of his wife's destruction. . . .

6. Imagine that you are directing a film version of one of the set texts. Choose any scene and discuss how you will film it, including all the decisions made in converting the text to the screen.

King Lear

. . .

The scene interpreted below is from *King Lear* - as a cinematic exercise it departs quite radically from convention and owes something to

Marowitz[24] and also to Derek Jarman's recent cinema version of Christopher Marlowe's play, *Edward II*. The scene is Act IV, Scene v - where Edgar leads the blind Gloucester to the top of a pretend cliff at Dover. However I have turned the play into an overtly, anti-capitalist political satire - with the already present hints of humour in the text exaggerated to comic proportions. The scene will resemble one found in Beckett's *Waiting for Godot* in the characters of Pozzo and Lucky.

The setting will be contemporary London – with Lear the former head of a multi-million-pound international business empire. His attempts to divide the company equally between his three daughters are thwarted by the two eldest, Regan and Goneril, fighting amongst themselves and turning on the younger Cordelia, and subsequently Lear himself is thrown out of the building which is also the family home. The 'wilderness' which Lear is cast out into are the streets of London itself. Powerless amid so many people, Lear feels unknown, anonymous, until he goes insane. Lear is depicted as reduced to that of the plight of many thousands of homeless people – forced to beg to survive.

The opening sequence of the scene will show the blind Gloucester and Edgar (also both in beggar's clothes) leading him not to the precipice of a pretend cliff - which Edgar has him believe - but rather to the very real fountains at Trafalgar Square. The action will take place at night. The precipice which Gloucester believes to be the edge of the cliff is merely the lip of the wall surrounding the fountain's shallow pool. When he jumps forward, believing he is falling to his death, he lands knee-deep in water – whereupon Edgar emerges and fishes him out. The lighting must be dramatic here to exaggerate the irony involved. Close-up shots of Gloucester's face as he prepares to jump also heighten audience response - simultaneously and paradoxically, of pity and laughter: laughter, as we stare into the face of a figure of ridicule - coupled with sadness at a half-soaked man's vain attempt at suicide. A long camera shot of Gloucester as he stands in the pool not knowing what to do will be juxtaposed with short sequences of couples laughing as they walk past. Gloucester's gouged eye-sockets stare blankly ahead.

A distant camera shot showing Gloucester in dark profile moves in slowly closer until the camera is behind him – close now – showing him twitching and shivering with his shadow cast long across the pool – which is shimmering with streetlights reflecting like eyes in the water.

Edgar intervenes and pulls him out, keeping up the pretence that he has fallen to the bottom of the cliff and miraculously survived 'From the dread summit of this chalky bourn./ Look up a-height. The shrill-gorged lark so far / Cannot be seen or heard. Do but look up' (IV.v. 57–9).

Suggested Further Topics

1. Choose a short scene and write a screenplay. Include a brief critical introduction.

2. With reference to one play, compare and contrast screen representations of gender, violence or race.

3. Examine the impact of one of the following (in one or more screen versions) on one of Shakespeare's plays: cinematic codes, language codes, visual codes, non-linguistic codes, cultural codes (see pp. 5–7).

4. Consider the reasons behind a director's choice of a particular play for a film.

5. Evaluate a filmography of one of Shakespeare's plays.

6. Consider the impact of a screen addition to Shakespeare.

Group Work

1. Break into groups of four or five. Design and then video a scene from a Shakespeare play. Be certain to assign roles of actors, director and cameraman/woman. The videos will be played back at a plenary discussion.

2. Consider a film of Shakespeare either in production or about to be released. Discuss reasons why the play was chosen and how it can be made to appeal to a contemporary audience.

Appendix 2: Evaluations

1. Choose a critical book or essay on one of Shakespeare's plays and compare it to a scene/sequence from the same play on screen (produced in the same period, that is, within six years). Discuss the ideological assumptions underlying the critic's account and the director's version of the play.

1. This student has made a promising start, but is not quite there. Clearly, there is a recognition that the text is reconstructed in critical accounts just as it is in a film adaptation; there is indication here of a growing critical response to criticisms of the play and the writer writes in his or her own voice rather than merely parroting the critic, which is all to often the case in undergraduate essays. However, there is a tendency to generalise. The critical approach adopted by these two 1960s readings could have been more clearly identified or described; it would have been helpful, too, to indicate how these readings differ from more recent readings of the play. Transitions from one observation to the next were often hard to follow. The approach is somewhat patronising, assuming a knowledge of critic/adapter's intentions which, of course, cannot be demonstrated.

    Although this work has certain defects, credit must be given for the promise it shows.

2. This is a better response to the topic; it is more challenging to evaluate a more contemporary text and the level of difficulty here is higher than the preceding analysis. More emphasis on audience expectation would have provided a fuller picture and the writer could have spelled out more clearly why Branagh celebrates his construction of Shakespearean community values while Howard attacks them. Although the writer identifies the differences

between the two texts, there is little attempt to provide reasons for these differences. Why is it necessary for Branagh to reverse Howard's reading of Beatrice, from that of victim to victor?

This piece demonstrates the different requirements of critic and film adapter and, as such, is an admirably comprehensive reading of the play text. When we compare it to the first essay, we can see how, in the 1960s, literary criticism and film adaptation of Shakespeare were more clearly aligned than they are in the 1990s.

2. Compare and contrast representations of sexuality in one play by Shakespeare with a film/televisual adaptation of the same text.

1. Although this piece is full of ideas it often disappointedly confuses gender and sexuality and therefore does not entirely address the topic. There is also an unfortunate tendency to blindly defend Branagh and Shakespeare (that is, without considering alternative views), making the argument overly subjective. Nonetheless the linking of sexuality with class is illuminating and in hindsight, this should have provided the focus for the piece. Once again, the writer's awareness of the differences between play text and film reflects a sound comprehension of the play.

2. This is a surprising choice of play for this topic – but the writer shows that this can be done and deserves credit for an unusual and, at times, convincing response. What is missing is a recognition that the discussion is about interpolations to the text; and, as such, fails to be a comparison of play and film, as required. The essay would have profited from some consideration of male sexuality in Shakespeare's *Henry V* and the ways in which they are reproduced and/or distorted by Branagh in order to appeal to a 1980s audience. It is often difficult to know what is meant in assertions such as that in Shakespeare 'men are unusually tactile by our twentieth-century standards'. Credit must be given for initiative and enthusiasm, but the piece is brought down substantially by an ultimate failure to compare film and play text.

3. Compare and contrast representations of nationality in a play text and film/televisual text(s) of the same play.

This is a sophisticated, well-informed response to the topic, although it is crying out for close analyses. In comparing the two film versions, the writer reflects on similarities rather than differences and this results in conclusions which are rather disappointing. It is all too obvious that the two directors/actors use *Henry V* as a vehicle for self-promotion; a more interesting approach would have been to look at how these different constructions of masculinity appeal to different perceptions of nationalism in the1940s and 1980s.

4. Compare two or more screen versions of a scene. You may consider the relevance of editing, casting, *mise en scène*, etc.

This is a very good close reading of the two films but misses the obvious point that camera angles and the Battle of Agincourt itself are *additions* to Shakespeare's text. It does seem to be the case that the most memorable features of an adaptation are the additions which enable the director to tie up loose ends and fill in the gaps in the text, allowing the viewer the opportunity to see more clearly the imposition of a meaning on to the text. The writer has a sharp critical instinct and, by looking at the two film versions of *Henry V*, becomes alerted to the ways in which discrete details, when taken together, can transform our reading of the text altogether.

5. Find a scene omitted from a film version(s) of a play and explain why it has been left out (for example, the boy's soliloquy in *Henry V*).

Parallels between a director's/writer's life and his or her work can never be proven and should be avoided; if it *is* necessary to make such a connection, then qualifications must be made. Nonetheless, the writer's awareness of the changes in the representation of Malcolm imply a sound comprehension of the play text and an awareness that the film of *Macbeth* is a manipulation of Shakespeare's text. However, it is not always clear how the evidence proves the point; for instance, how does Malcolm's offer of a drink to Macbeth reveal the former's weakness? This is a good start, but the writer needs to reflect more on the consequences of interpolations and omissions and get out of the habit of reading the adaptation as concealed biography.

6. Imagine that you are directing a film version of one of the set texts. Choose any scene and discuss how you will film it; including all the decisions made in converting the text to the screen.

Creative exercises such as this are almost always lively and reflect an engagement with the text which is rare in the more 'standard' under-graduate essays. It is clear from this exercise that the writer has read and reread the play in a way which would suit contemporary tastes, something which is undoubtedly part of the process of reading itself. The discussion should have included *why* this scene would suit this particular reading; this is undoubtedly a compelling reworking, but a fuller explanation of the particular audience this is aimed at would have improved the essay.

Notes

Preface

1. *The Guardian Friday Review,* 19 April 1996, p. 3.
2. 'The Crucible', *New Statesman and Society,* 28 February 1997, p. 43.
3. *The Novel and the Cinema* (Cranbury, NJ: Associated University Presses, 1975), pp. 222–6.

1 Shakespeare, Film and Violence: Doing Violence to Shakespeare

1. See Imelda Whelehan, 'Adaptations: The Contemporary Dilemmas', in *Adaptations: From Text to Screen, Screen to Text,* ed. Deborah Cartmell and Imelda Whelehan (London and New York: Routledge, 1999), pp. 3–22 for an account of previous work on film adaptations.
2. See Sharon Ouditt, 'Orlando: Coming Across the Divide', in Cartmell and Whelehan (eds.), *Adaptations,* pp. 145–56.
3. In *Film Form* (Cleveland and New York: Meridian, 1957), pp. 232–3.
4. *'Hamlet': The Film and the Play,* ed. Alan Dent (London: World Film Publications Ltd, 1948), p. 9.
5. *Biography This Week,* broadcast 9 November 1996, A&E.
6. *Classics and Trash: Traditions and Taboos in High Literature and Popular Modern Genres* (London and New York: Harvester Wheatsheaf, 1990), p. 123.
7. Ibid., p. 123.
8. *'Hamlet': The Film and the Play,* ed. Dent, p. 11.
9. For a discuss of adaptations and nostalgia, see R. Giddings, K.

Selby and C. Wensley, *Screening the Novel: The Theory and Practice of Literary Dramatization* (Basingstoke: Macmillan, 1990), p. 34.

10. See John O. Thompson, '"Vanishing"' Worlds: Film Adaptation and the Mystery of the Original', in *Pulping Fictions: Consuming Culture across the Literature/Media Divide*, ed. Deborah Cartmell, I. Q. Hunter, Heidi Kaye and Imelda Whelehan (London: Pluto, 1996), pp. 11–28. Thompson considers the desire to concretise, to make the literary text 'real'.

11. *Distinction: A Social Critique of the Judgement of Taste*, trans. Richard Nice (London and New York: Routledge & Kegan Paul, 1979) and *The Field of Cultural Production*, ed. Randal Johnson (Oxford: Polity Press, 1993).

12. *Reframing Culture: The Case of the Vitagraph Quality Films* (Princeton: Princeton University Press, 1993), p. 9.

13. *The Olive and the Sword* (Oxford University Press, 1944), p. 3. See Chapter 5, this volume.

14. Kenneth Branagh, *'Hamlet' by William Shakespeare: Screenplay, Introduction and Film Diary* (London: Chatto & Windus, 1996), p. v.

15. *How to Read a Film* (New York and Oxford: Oxford University Press, 1981), p. 219.

16. *Walking Shadows: Shakespeare in the National Film and Television Archive*, ed. Luke McKernan and Olwen Terris (London: National Film Theatre, 1994), p. 22.

17. *Novel to Film: An Introduction to the Theory of Adaptation* (Oxford: Clarendon Press, 1996), p. 23.

18. Ibid., p. 29 (my definitions). McFarlane defines cultural codes as 'involving all that information which has to do with how people live, or lived, at particular times and places'.

19. *The Essays of Virginia Woolf, Volume IV: 1924–1928*, ed. Andrew McNeillie (London: Hogarth, 1994), p. 350.

20. This is perhaps most noticeable in Disney films, such as *The Lion King*, where the evil Scar (the voice of Jeremy Irons) is distinguishable from the good lions by his English accent.

21. II.i.305. Unless otherwise cited, all quotations from Shakespeare are taken from *The Complete Works*, ed. Stanley Wells, Gary Taylor, John Jowett, and William Montgomery (Oxford: Clarendon Press, 1988).

22. In the same way, other inaccuracies are irritating, the most obvious the implication that *Romeo and Juliet* was entirely Shakespeare's brainchild. There is no reference to his source in the film.

23. *Walking Shadows: Shakespeare in the National Film and Television Archive*, p. 195.

24. *Titus Andronicus*, ed. Jonathan Bate (London and New York: Routledge, 1995), pp. 33–4, 3.

25. *The Culture of Violence: Tragedy and History* (Manchester: Manchester University Press, 1993), pp. 178–9.

26. Quoted in Roger Sales, *Christopher Marlowe* (London: Macmillan, 1991), p. 23.

27. See Foucault's discussion of the 'theatre of hell' in Michel Foucault, *Discipline and Punish: The Birth of the Prison*, trans. Alan Sheridan (Haromondsworth: Penguin, 1977).

28. *The Censure of a Loyall Subject*, quoted in Sales, *Christopher Marlowe*, pp. 27–8.

29. See D. J. Palmer, 'The unspeakable in pursuit of the uneatable: language and action in *Titus Andronicus*', *Critical Quarterly*, 14 (1972), 320–39.

30. The discussion of *King Lear* includes only the major English versions as they are the most accessible to students. Interestingly, however, Akira Kurosawa's free adaptation of *King Lear, Ran* (1985), leaves out the blinding episode, including it only as an event from the past, recalled but not shown.

31. These lines occur only in the Quarto text (xiv.104–5).

32. Jorgens, *Shakespeare on Film* (London and Bloomington: Indiana University Press, 1977), p. 161.

33. William P. Shaw, 'Violence and vision in Polanski's *Macbeth* and Brook's *Lear*', *Literature/Film Quarterly*, 4:4, 1986, 211–13, at pp. 211, 213.

34. *William Shakespeare* (Oxford: Blackwell, 1986), p. 3.

35. John Russell Taylor, *The Times*, 4 February 1972, p. 9.

2   Shakespeare, Film and Gender: Critical and Filmic Representations of *Hamlet*

1. 'The Making of *Henry V*', *Laurence Olivier's Henry V* (Lorrimer Publishing Ltd, New York, 1984).

2. See Chapter 5.

3. See, for example, the period 1995–96 in which each of these collections contains an article on Shakespeare and film: James C. Bulman, ed., *Shakespeare, Theory, and Performance* (1996), Deborah Barker and Ivo Kamps, eds, *Shakespeare and Gender: A History* (1996), Heather Kerr, Robin Eaden and Madge Mitton, eds., *Shakespeare: World Views* (1996) and Robert F. Willson Jr., ed., *Entering the Maze: Shakespeare's Art of Beginning* (1995). The Shakespeare in Performance series, published by Manchester University Press, also includes major sections on Shakespeare on screen (see, for example, Anthony B. Dawson, *Hamlet*, 1995).

4. (London and New York: Routledge), p. 1.

5. In *Walking Shadows: Shakespeare in the National Film and Television Archive*, ed. Luke McKernan and Olwen Terris (London: National Film Theatre, 1994), pp. 921–6.

6. See Chapter 4.

7. Bernice Kliman, *Hamlet: Film, Television and Audio Performance* (London: Associated University Presses, 1988), p. 297.

8. *Shakespeare, Cinema and Society* (Manchester: Manchester University Press, 1989), p. 4.

9. *Critical Practice* (London and New York: Methuen, 1980), p. 20.

10. E. D. Pribram, ed., *Female Spectators* (London: Verso, 1988), p. 6.

11. See Chapter 5.

12. Kliman, *Hamlet*, p. 26.

13. *Shakespearean Tragedy* (1904), rpt. in John Jump, ed., *Shakespeare: Hamlet* (London: Macmillan, 1968), p. 39.

14. 'Hamlet' (1919), rpt. in Jump, ed., *Shakespeare: Hamlet*, p. 39.

15. Spurgeon, *Shakespeare's Imagery and What it Tells Us* (1935, rpt. Cambridge: Cambridge University Press, 1993), p. 316.

16. Laurence Olivier, *Confessions of an Actor: An Autobiography* (New York: Weidenfeld & Nicolson, 1982), p. 79.

17. Ernest Jones, *Hamlet and Oedipus* (1949; rpt. New York: Norton, 1976), p. 86.

18. Ibid., p. 84.

19. J. Dover Wilson, *What Happens in Hamlet* (Cambridge: Cambridge University Press, 1937), p. 131.

20. Ibid., p. 131.

21. I am grateful to Anne Marie Beller for calling my attention to this image.

22. Olivier cunningly replaces the irony implicit in Ophelia's 'O, what a noble mind is here o'erthrown' in the play text; cruelly, it is Ophelia's 'noble mind' which is in peril, not Hamlet's.

23. *The Film 'Hamlet': A Record of its Production*, ed. Brenda Cross (London: Saturn Press), p. 56.

24. Anthony B. Dawson, *Shakespeare in Performance: 'Hamlet'* (Manchester: Manchester University Press, 1995), pp. 182–3.

25. Maynard Mack, *The World of 'Hamlet'* (1952), in Jump, ed., *Shakespeare: Hamlet*, p. 105.

26. Kliman, *Hamlet*, p. 91.

27. Jan Kott, *Shakespeare Our Contemporary* (1964), in Jump, ed., *Shakespeare: Hamlet*, pp. 197–9.

28. *The Literary Review*, 22:4 (1979), 385–90.

29. John Bayley, *Shakespeare and Tragedy* (London: Routledge & Kegan Paul, 1981), p. 173.

30. Surveying the British Film Institute holding of stills for the Olivier production, I was struck at how many there were of the making of Ophelia's death – a scene unfortunately rather laughable in the Olivier film. It was obviously put together with enormous care in its reconstruction of the famous Millais portrait where Ophelia is portrayed in death as a virgin ready to greet her lover. Roger Furse's comments in 'Designing the Film of *Hamlet*', in *'Hamlet: The Film and the Play* (1948), reveal the care taken in attempting to reconstruct the Millais portrait: 'I think of the hours I spent paddling about in leaky waders, having started from London at five in the morning in order to get the right angle of light; of the plastic petticoat worn under the dress to make it float; of the cotton leads attached to the flowers, which otherwise would have drifted too fast down the stream' (p. 36).

31. Pribram, ed., *Female Spectators*, p. 1.

32. Jardine, *Still Harping on Daughters: Women and Drama in the Age of Shakespeare* (1983; 2nd edn. New York, London and Toronto: Harvester, 1989), p. 73.

33. Dusinberre, *Shakespeare and the Nature of Women* (London: Macmillan, 1975), p. 5.

34. Elaine Showalter, 'Representing Ophelia: Women, Madness, and the Responsibilities of Feminist Criticism', in *Hamlet, Case Studies in Contemporary Criticism*, ed. Susanne L. Wofford (Boston and New York: St Martin's Press and Macmillan, 1994), pp. 220–40, at p. 233.

35. T. Eagleton, *William Shakespeare* (Oxford: Blackwell, 1986), p. 74.

36. See Doug Stenberg, 'Shakespearean motifs in *The Lion King*', *Shakespeare Bulletin* 14:2 (1996), 36–8. *The Lion King*, in its account of a young prince coming of age, can be seen also as a loose adaptation of the *Henry IV* plays. In fact, Shakespeare seems to be behind a number of Disney productions in the 1990s. The sequel to *The Lion King, Simba's Pride* (1998), is a happy version of *Romeo and Juliet*; *Aladdin* (1992) features a parrot, named Iago, whose goading of his master is surely based on Shakespeare's Iago, and the heroine of *Mulan* (1998), who cross-dresses and falls in love while in disguise, bears a striking resemblance to figures such as Viola in *Twelfth Night*.

37. 13 February, 26–7.

38. *Entertainment Weekly*, http://us.imdb.com/search.html, 19 September 1996.

39. In fact Branagh pays tribute, in his introduction to the screenplay, to Jacobi's Hamlet which, Branagh claims, inspired his own career. '*Hamlet' by William Shakespeare: Screenplay, Introduction and Film Diary* (London: Chatto & Windus, 1996), p. v.

40. Ibid., pp. 187–8.

41. According to Anny Crunelle Vanrigh, 'All the World's a Screen: Transcoding in Branagh's *Hamlet*', in *Hamlet on Film*, ed. Holger Klein and Dimiter Daphinoff, *Shakespeare Yearbook* Vol. 8 (Lewiston: Edwin Mellen Press, 1997), pp. 349–69, the 'mirror in Branagh becomes the metaphor of the transcoding of play into film. It is also very adequately a cinematic, visual transposition of the dramatic, aural convention of the soliloquy' (p. 358).

42. *Hamlet* (London: Methuen, 1982), p. 146.

43. 'Watching *Hamlet* Watching: Lacan, Shakespeare and the Mirror/ Stage', *Alternative Shakespeares*, Vol. 2., ed. Terence Hawkes (London and New York: Routledge, 1996), pp. 216–37, at p. 235.

44. Cynthia J. Fuchs, 'The Buddy Politic', in *Screening the Male*, ed. Steven Cohen and Ina Rae Hark (London and New York: Routledge, 1993), pp. 194–210, p. 203.

45. (London: Routledge, 1996).

46. *The Independent Tabloid*, 13 February 1997, p. 5.

3   Shakespeare, Film and Sexuality: Politically Correct Sexuality in Film Adaptations of *Romeo and Juliet* and *Much Ado About Nothing*

1. *The Times*, 30 January 1994.
2. *The Observer*, 30 January 1994, p. 18.
3. *Shakespeare's Bawdy* (1947; 3rd edn. rpt. London and New York: Routledge, 1990), p. ix.
4. Ibid., pp. 11–12.
5. Ibid., p. 14.
6. Quoted by Martin Kettle in the *Guardian*, 22 January 1994, p. 23.
7. The *Guardian*, 27 January 1994, p. 20.
8. See note 2 above. In spite of what seems to be universal acknowledgement in the media that Shakespeare has little to say about homoeroticism, recent criticism of Shakespeare indicates the reverse. See, for example, Elaine Hobby, 'My Affection Hath an Unknown Bottom': Homosexuality and the Teaching of *As You Like It*', in *Shakespeare in the Changing Curriculum*, ed. Lesley Aers and Nigel Wheale (London: Routledge, 1991) and Valerie Traub, *Desire and Anxiety: Circulations of Sexuality in Shakespearean Drama* (London: Routledge, 1992).
9. The *Guardian*, 23 January 1994, p. 19.
10. *Desire and Anxiety*, p. 21.
11. Lisa Jardine in the *Guardian*, 23 January 1994, p. 19 and Alan Sinfield, *Council for College and University English*, No.1, 1994.
12. See notes 2 and 5 above.
13. John Russell Taylor, *The Times*, 5 March 1968, p. 7.
14. *Shakespeare on Film* (London and Bloomington: Indiana University Press, 1977), p. 85.
15. There are three types of gaze as first described by Laura Mulvey which involve men looking at women: the look of the camera in which the male director voyeuristically gazes at women, the gaze of the men within the film and the gaze of the male spectator of the film. ('Visual pleasure and narrative cinema', *Screen*, 16:3 (1975), 6–19). Here the gaze is interpreted to include women looking at men, men looking at men and women looking at women.
16. According to Zeffirelli, this episode had to go as if Romeo 'was a murderer – "ugly boy, ugly boy!" It wouldn't have worked.' This

passage is quoted by Robert Hapgood, 'The Artistry of Franco Zeffirelli', in *Shakespeare the Movie: Popularizing the Plays on Film, TV, and Video*, ed. Lynda E. Boose and Richard Burt (London: Routledge, 1997), pp. 80–94.

17. But as Michel Foucault has argued in *The History of Sexuality*, the sovereign alone has power over life and death; in this sense, the suicides of Romeo and Juliet, resulting from their sexual transgression, can be seen as the supreme form of opposition, a usurpation of sovereign power. In *The History of Sexuality*, trans. Robert Hurley (1979; rpt. Harmondsworth: Penguin, 1984), Michel Foucault outlines how the 'right' to one's body – in the fullest sense – ultimately belongs to the sovereign in the early modern period.

18. *Coming of Age in Shakespeare* (London and New York: Methuen, 1981) p. 144.

19. Zeffirelli emphasises Juliet's increasing independence in line with Coppelia Kahn's reading in 'Coming of Age in Verona', in *The Woman's Part: Feminist Criticism of Shakespeare*, ed. C. R. S. Lenz, G. Greene and C. Thomas (Champaign: University of Illinois Press, 1980), pp. 171–93, where Juliet's control of the dagger is vital to her resistance of patriarchal pressures. Romeo, too, is largely liberated from patriarchal claims; as Peter S. Donaldson notes in his analysis of Zeffirelli's film, unlike the other males, Romeo is only once associated with the sword/phallus metaphor in his duel with Tybalt (*Shakespearean Films/Shakespearean Directors*, Boston and London: Unwin Hyman, 1990, p. 161).

20. *The Independent Tabloid*, 27 March 1997, pp. 4–5.

21. Rebecca Fowler, *The Times*, 29 August 1993.

22. Iain Johnstone, *The Times*, 15 August 1993.

23. 'The importance of being ordinary', *Sight and Sound*, 3:9 (September 1993), p. 19.

24. *The Times*, 29 August 1993.

25. *Much Ado About Nothing: The Making of the Movie* (New York: Norton, 1993), p. xvi.

26. Catherine Bennett, the *Guardian*, 7 August 1993, p. 16.

27. *The Times*, 25 May 1994.

28. For an experienced filmgoer, Don John may recall the gay character played by Keanu Reeves in an earlier Shakespeare film, Gus Van Sant's *My Own Private Idaho* (1991). This would serve to rein-

force an implicit association between evil and homosexuality
drawn in Branagh's film.

29. "'Your answer, sir, is cinematical": Kenneth Branagh's *Much Ado
About Nothing', Shakespeare Bulletin*, 12 (1994), 42–5, at p. 44.

30. *Much Ado About Nothing: The Making of the Movie*, p. xi.

31. *Amoretti*, Sonnet 67, ll. 11–14. In *Edmund Spenser's Poetry*,
selected and edited by Hugh MacLean and Anne Lake Prescott
(1968; 3rd edn. rpt. New York and London: Norton, 1993).

32. See Lynda Boose, 'Scolding brides and bridling scolds: taming the
woman's unruly member', *Shakespeare Quarterly*, 42 (1991),
179–213.

33. See Lisa Jardine, 'Shrewd or Shrewish', in *Still Harping on
Daughters* (Brighton: Harvester, 1983), pp. 121–33.

34. Interestingly, these lines are attributed to Leonato in both the
Quarto and Folio.

4 Shakespeare, Film and Race: Screening *Othello* and *The Tempest*

1. (Ithaca and London: Cornell University Press, 1993).

2. *How to Read a Film* (New York and Oxford: Oxford University
Press, 1981), p. 225.

3. The word 'black' is being used here, as Homi Bhabha has defined
his usage, 'not to deny [racially marginalized groups'] diversity but
to audaciously announce the important artifice of cultural identity
and its difference'('Remembering Fanon', foreword to F. Fanon,
Black Skin, White Masks, London: Pluto Press, 1986, p. xxvi).

4. *Gender, Race, Renaissance Drama* (Manchester: Manchester University Press, 1989).

5. Ibid., pp. 40–1.

6. With Harry V. Jaffa, *Shakespeare's Politics* (1964; rpt. University of
Chicago Press, 1987), pp. 61–2.

7. The *Observer Review*, 9 October 1994, p. 6.

8. The *Guardian*, 29 June 1994, p. 22.

9. Introduction: 'Friday on the Potomac', *Race-ing Justice, En-
gendering Power: Essays on Anita Hill, Clarence Thomas and the
Construction of Social Reality*, ed. Toni Morrison (London: Chatto
& Windus, 1993), p. xiv.

10. For instance, Charles Higham, *The Films of Orson Welles* (Berkeley: University of California Press, 1970), p. 142. Higham points out the production problems with the film. Cloutier, for example, was the fourth Desdemona on the set – her voice was dubbed by another actress.

11. See William Empson, 'Honest in Othello' (1951) and F. R. Leavis, 'Diabolic Intellect and the Noble Hero' (1952), both reprinted in *Shakespeare: Casebook Series Othello*, ed. John Wain (1971; 2nd edn rpt. Basingstoke: Macmillan, 1994), pp. 98–122, 123–46.

12. See, for instance, Philip Butcher, 'Othello's Racial Identity', *Shakespeare Quarterly*, 111 (1952), 243–9 and M. R. Ridley below, note 15.

13. *The Times*, 30 September 1965, p. 16.

14. This quotation (from John Simon, 'Pearl throwing free style', in Charles W. Eckert ed., *Focus on Shakespearean Films* (Englewood Cliffs: Prentice Hall, 1972, p. 155) was suggested by Timothy Murray in *Like a Film: Ideological Fantasy on Screen, Camera and Canvas* (London and New York: Routledge, 1993), p. 111.

15. Quoted in the Arden Edition *Othello*, ed. M. R. Ridley (1959; rpt. London: Methuen, 1982), p. li.

16. Ibid., p. li.

17. 'Race-ing Othello, Re-engendering White-Out', in *Shakespeare the Movie: Popularizing the Plays on Film, TV, and Video*, ed. Lynda E. Boose and Richard Burt (New York and London: Routledge, 1997), pp. 23–44, at p. 30.

18. There are also lesser-known films, one directed by Liz White (1966; commercially released in 1980) and another adaptation directed by Ted Lange (1990), where both Othello and Iago are played by black actors. I am grateful to José Ramón Díaz-Fernández for drawing these to my attention.

19. Rhoda Koenig, *Punch*, 13 October 1989. This passage was suggested by Barbara Hodgdon ('Race-ing Othello', p. 33), who also uses the Simpson trial as an analogue to white readings of the filmed play. Strangely, she restricts herself to the two late 1980s versions – when the Parker version – contemporary to the trial – demonstrates clear parallels. Hodgdon implies throughout her discussion that Othello *must* be a black man on screen. In *The Shakespeare Trade: Performances & Appropriations* (Philadelphia: University of Pennsylvania Press, 1998), the Parker film is tagged

on to her piece ('Race-ing Othello', pp. 39–73); the film is read as post-O. J. (even though it was in production during the trial) and, seemingly approving of the performance of Othello, blame is attached to the representation of Desdemona: Parker's 'strategy enhances [Iago's] control of the cinematic apparatus and its ability to objectify and blame women – even, as the poster image of "Adam and Evil" suggests, to re-mark them with his own actions and desires, turning them into substitutes of himself' (p. 70).

20. '"Othello Was a White Man"': Properties of Race on Shakespeare's Stage', in *Alternative Shakespeares*, Vol. 2, ed. Terence Hawkes (London and New York: Routledge, 1996), pp. 192–215, at p. 215.

21. See Richard Harwell, '*Gone with the Wind' as Book and Film* (Columbia: University of South Carolina Press, 1983).

22. 'Shakespearian Transformations', in *Shakespeare and National Culture*, ed. John J. Joughin (Manchester and New York: Manchester University Press, 1997), pp. 109–41, at p. 139.

23. *Time Out*, 14–21 February 1996.

24. Tim De Lisle, 'A Case of Less is Moor', *Independent on Sunday*, 21 January 1996, p. 17.

25. John Dargie, '*Othello*', *L.A. Weekly*, 27 December 1995, p. 67.

26. A. Walker, the *Evening Standard*, 15 February 1996.

27. Ibid.

28. Ibid.

29. *Variety*, 11–17 December 1995.

30. Bhabha, 'The other question: difference, discrimination and the discourse of colonialism', in F. Barker et al., eds., *Literature, Politics and Theory* (London: Methuen, 1986), p. 159.

31. (1954; rpt. London: Methuen, 1979), p. xli.

32. Jarman, *Dancing Ledge* (1984; rpt. London: Quartet, 1991), p. 206.

33. In fact, it's difficult to see anything in the film which – as John Collick claims in his reading of Jarman's film – interrogates accepted attitudes towards sexuality. See *Shakespeare, Cinema and Society* (Manchester: Manchester University Press, 1989), pp. 98–106.

34. Quoted in Kate Chedgzoy, *Shakespeare's Queer Children: Sexual Politics and Contemporary Culture* (Manchester: Manchester University Press, 1995), p. 202.

35. See ibid., p. 201.

36. "'This thing of darkness I acknowledge mine'": *The Tempest* and the discourse of colonialism', in *Political Shakespeare*, ed. Jonathan Dollimore and Alan Sinfield (1985; 2nd edn. rpt. Manchester: Manchester University Press, 1994) pp. 48–71, at p. 62.

37. 'Veritable negroes and circumcized dogs: racial Disturbances in Shakespeare', in *Shakespeare in the Changing Curriculum*, ed. L. Aers and N. Wheale (London: Routledge, 1991), pp. 108–24, at p. 114.

38. *The Tempest*, ed. Stephen Orgel (Oxford and New York: Oxford University Press, 1987), Introduction, p. 36.

39. 'Whose Things of Darkness? Reading/Representing *The Tempest* in South Africa After April 1994', in *Shakespeare and National Culture, ed.* Joughin, pp. 142–70, p. 160.

40. *Dancing Ledge*, p. 183.

41. Jarman's admiration of controversial gay dancer Michael Clark is recorded in his autobiography; the title is inspired by Jarman's impression of Clark's dancing. The choice of Clark for Caliban is possibly one of many footnotes to Jarman in *Prospero's Books*.

42. John Gielgud, an extract from his autobiography, in the *Guardian*, 22 August 1991, p. 21.

43. Gilbert Adair, the *Guardian*, 5 September 1991, p. 26.

44. See above, p. 80.

45. *Shakespeare, Cinema and Society*, p. 10.

46. *Dancing Ledge*, p. 186.

47. The shooting script was obtained from Castle Rock.

5   Shakespeare, Film and Nationalism: *Henry V*

1. See Victoria McKee, 'Based on an original idea by William Shakespeare', *The Independent Weekend*, 20 April 1996, p. 6.

2. What follows is an expanded version of two articles: my contribution to I. Whelehan and D. Cartmell, 'Through a Painted Curtain: Laurence Olivier's *Henry V'*, in *War Culture: Social Change and Changing Experience in World War Two*, ed. P. Kirkham and D. Thoms (London: Lawrence & Wishart, 1995) and D. Cartmell, 'The Shakespeare Flashback: Kenneth Branagh's Shakespeare', in D. Cartmell, I. Q. Hunter, H. Kaye and I. Whelehan, eds., *Pulping*

Fictions: Consuming Culture across the Literature/Film Divide (London: Pluto, 1996).

3. This view is typified by Sara Manson Deats, who regards Olivier's *Henry V* as in all ways positive, the mirror opposite of Branagh's version. 'Rabbits and ducks: Olivier, Branagh and *Henry V*', *Literature/Film Quarterly*, 20 (1992), 284–93.

4. *Shakespeare, Cinema and Society* (Manchester: Manchester University Press, 1989), pp. 47–9.

5. *Shakespeare Recyled: The Making of Historical Drama* (New York and London: Harvester Wheatsheaf, 1992), p. 22.

6. *The Olive and the Sword* (Oxford: Oxford University Press, 1944), pp. 3, 29.

7. *Shakespeare's History Plays* (1944; rpt. London: Chatto & Windus, 1964), p. 315.

8. *Shakespeare* (1939; rpt. Garden City: Doubleday, 1953), p. 144.

9. 'Henry the Fifth', *Scrutiny*, ix (1941), 364. Traversi's article represents the only account of *Henry V* in *Scrutiny* during the war years.

10. '*Henry IV* Part 1', *Scrutiny*, 15 (1947).

11. Una Ellis Fermor, *The Frontiers of Drama* (London: Methuen, 1945).

12. See Anthony Davies, 'Shakespeare and the media of film, radio and television: a retrospect', *Shakespeare Survey*, 39 (1986), 1–11.

13. Laurence Olivier, *On Acting* (London: Weidenfeld & Nicolson, 1986), p. 190.

14. Jorgens in *Shakespeare on Film* (London and Bloomington: Indiana University Press, 1977), considers three types of cinematic modes: the theatrical mode (which uses film as a transparent medium), the 'realistic mode' (which shifts the emphasis from actors to actors in a setting) and the filmic mode (a poetic rendering). In his study of the Olivier film, Anthony Davies, in *Filming Shakespeare's Plays: The Adaptations of Laurence Olivier, Orson Welles, Peter Brook and Akira Kurosawa* (Cambridge: Cambridge University Press, 1988), examines three levels of time in the film: Renaissance time, medieval time and universal time. He suggests that the shift from 'narrative congruency to narrative co-operation between chorus and camera' achieves a spatial concentration which reveals 'universal time' (p. 29). Lorne M.

Buchman in *Still in Movement: Shakespeare on Screen* (Oxford: Oxford University Press, 1991), Chapter 5, considers the dialectics of filmic and theatrical spaces and discusses the manipulation of three types of space in Olivier's film: theatre space (the Globe theatre section), the self-consciously illusionistic space (from Southampton to Agincourt) and the expansive space of cinematic movement (in the Battle of Agincourt).

15. The careful reconstruction of the fifteenth-century illuminations is discussed by Dale Silviria, *Laurence Olivier and the Art of Film Making* (Rutherford: Fairleigh Dickinson University Press, 1985).

16. In G. Mast and M. Cohen, eds., *Film Theory and Criticism* (Oxford: Oxford University Press, 1974), p. 336.

17. *English Our English: The New Orthodoxy Examined* (London: Centre for Policy Studies, 1987).

18. *The Olive and the Sword*, pp. 39, 40.

19. Jorgens, in *Shakespeare on Film*, examines the visual motif of gates in his analysis of Olivier's *Henry V.*

20. Harry M. Geduld, *Filmguide to Henry V* (Bloomington and London: Indiana University Press, 1973), p. 46.

21. *The Times*, 5 October 1989.

22. It is, nonetheless, worth noting that when comparing Branagh's *Henry V* to Olivier's, our first impression is to note the inclusions, but compared to the play text, as Robert Lane outlines in '"When blood is their argument": class, character, and historymaking in Shakespeare's and Branagh's *Henry V*', *English Literary History*, 61 (1994), 27–52, Branagh, like Olivier before him, evades a number of chinks in Henry's ideological armour, among them:

    1. Pistol's remarks to his wife that 'oaths are straws' (II.iii.51).

    2. Fluellen's historical analogy of Alexander and Henry in which Alexander killed his best friend (IV.vii).

    3. Much of Henry's disclaimer of responsibility for war to Williams (IV.1).

    4. Pistol's ransom scene (IV.iv).

    5. The boy's complaint that Pistol survives while Bardolf and Nym were hanged (IV.iv.70–4).

    6. Cutting much of Williams's attack on Henry (IV.i.197–201) and eliminating the scene in which Henry refers to Williams's challenge and offers him payment (IV.viii).

23. 'Invisible Bullets', in Greenblatt, *Shakespearean Negotiations: The*

Circulation of Social Energy in Renaissance England (Berkeley: University of California Press, 1988), p. 56.

24. In *Alternative Shakespeares,* ed. John Drakakis (London: Methuen, 1985), pp. 206–27, at p. 226.

25. The message is 'but since men are a contemptible lot, and would not keep their promises to you, you too need not keep yours to them', trans. Mark Musa (New York: St Martin's Press, 1964), Chapter XVII, p. 145.

26. *The Times,* 5 October 1989.

27. Critics have often referred to the dead boy as 'anonymous', yet it is Christian Bale, the actor who plays the boy of the tavern company. The mistake is easily made as it is, strangely, hard to identify Bale in the long tracking shot of Branagh carrying the dead boy across the battlefield. See K. Branagh, *Beginning* (New York: Norton, 1989), p. 236.

28. *Shakespeare Recycled,* pp. 191–2.

29. There are, nonetheless, a few unintentional seams in the film's realism, such as Branagh's 1980s hair style (which in no way resembles the famous crop of Henry V); Branagh's hair seems to have been washed and blow-dried in between cuts of the Harfleur sequence. At one point it is muddied and flattened, while a few moments later it has been restored to its earlier glory.

30. See Holderness, *Shakespeare Recycled,* p. 200.

31. 'A Tale of Two Branaghs: *Henry V,* Ideology, and the Mekong Agincourt', in *Shakespeare Left and Right,* ed. Ivo Kamps (London: Routledge,1991), p. 270. See also Branagh's *Hamlet* as a 'buddy film', above, pp. 36–8.

32. Lisa Buckingham, the *Guardian,* 30 January 1990, p. 9.

33. *Beginning,* p. 141.

34. Martin Kettle, the *Guardian,* 22 January 1994, p. 23.

35. 'Kenneth Branagh's *Henry V:* The Gilt [Guilt] in the Crown Re-Examined', *Comparative Drama,* 24 (1990), 173–8.

36. 23 February 1990, 116–117, at p. 116

37. This is also noted by Peter Donaldson, 'Taking on Shakespeare: Kenneth Branagh's *Henry V', Shakespeare Quarterly,* 42:1 (1991), 60–70, at p. 63.

38. *Humanist,* July/August 1990, 43–4.

39. 'Shakespeare in the National Curriculum', in Lesley Aers and

Nigel Wheale, *Shakespeare in the Changing Curriculum* (London: Routledge, 1991), pp. 30–9.

40. 'Re-loading the canon: Shakespeare and the study guides', *Shakespeare and National Culture*, ed. John J. Joughin (Manchester and New York: Manchester University Press, 1997), pp. 42–57, at p. 49.

41. 'NATO's pharmacy: Shakespeare by prescription', in Joughin, ed., *Shakespeare and National Culture*, pp. 58–80, at p. 71.

42. From the Preface to *The Taming of the Shrew*, ed. Michael Fynes-Clinton and Perry Mills (Cambridge: Cambridge University Press, 1992).

43. The *Daily Mirror,* 1 September 1997.

44. John Drakakis, 'Shakespeare in Quotations', in *Studying British Cultures: An Introduction,* ed. Susan Bassnett (London and New York: Routledge, 1997), pp. 152–72, at p. 157.

45. See note 6 above.

6 Conclusions

1. See Introduction, pp. 3–4.

2. Interview on Film Education, *Screening Shakespeares: 'Romeo and Juliet'*, video (1996).

3. Deborah Cartmell, 'Zeffirelli's Shakespeare', in *The Cambridge Companion to Shakespeare on Screen,* ed. Russell Jackson (Cambridge: Cambridge University Press, forthcoming). See also Paul Wells's analysis of the animated Shakespeare series in '"Thou art Translated": Analysing Animated Adaptation', in *Adaptations: From Text to Screen, Screen to Text,* ed. D. Cartmell and I. Whelehan (London: Routledge, 1999), pp. 199–213.

4. This is discussed by Emma Smith, '"Remember Me": The Gaumont–Hepworth Hamlet (1913)', in *'Hamlet' on Film, The Shakespeare Yearbook,* Vol. 8 (1997), pp. 110–24.

5. See Douglas Lanier, '"Drowning the Book": *Prospero's Books* and the Textual Shakespeare', in *New Casebooks: Shakespeare on Film,* ed. Robert Shaughnessy (Basingstoke and London: Macmillan, 1998), pp. 173–95.

6. Ibid., p. 190.

7. The song is based on Christina Rossetti's poem, 'A Christmas Carol'.
8. The *Guardian*, 30 January, 1999, 'Saturday Review', p. 2.
9. 'Radical Potentiality and Institutional Closure: Shakespeare in Film and Television', in *Political Shakespeare,* ed. Jonathan Dollimore and Alan Sinfield (Manchester: Manchester University Press, 1985), pp. 206–25, at p. 210.
10. Examiner's report dated 1997, p. 207.
11. 'Bardolatry: or, The Cultural Materialist's Guide to Stratford-upon-Avon', *The Shakespeare Myth,* ed. Graham Holderness (Manchester: Manchester University Press, 1988), pp. 2–15.

Appendix 1: Student Exercises

1. Lorne M. Buchman, *Still in Movement: Shakespeare on Screen,* (Oxford: Oxford University Press, 1991), p. 33.
2. Ibid.
3. Introduction, *Romeo and Juliet* (Harmondsworth: Penguin, 1967).
4. Brooke, *Shakespeare's Early Tragedies* (London: Methuen, 1968), p. 87.
5. Ibid., p. 81.
6. Ibid., p. 106.
7. Jack Jorgens, *Shakespeare on Film* (Bloomington and London: Indiana University Press, 1977), p. 86.
8. Brooke, *Shakespeare's Early Tragedies,* p. 106.
9. Kenneth Branagh, *Much Ado About Nothing: The Making of the Movie* (New York: Norton, 1993), p. xvi.
10. *Evelina* (Oxford: Oxford University Press, 1982), p. 164.
11. Peter Holland, 'Shakespeare's Performances in England', *Shakespeare Survey,* 47 (1994), 181–208.
12. Cynthia Fuchs, 'The Buddy Politic', in *Screening the Male,* ed. S. Conan and I. R. Hark (London: Routledge, 1993), p. 194.
13. Ibid.
14. J. E. Howard and M. F. O'Connor, *Shakespeare Reproduced: The Text in History and Ideology* (London: Routledge, 1989), p. 7.
15. Raymond Williams, in J. Dollimore and A. Sinfield, eds., *Political Shakespeare* (Manchester: Manchester University Press, 1985), p. 154.

16. Ibid. p. 157.
17. *Shakespeare, Cinema and Society* (Manchester: Manchester University Press, 1989), p. 4.
18. Robert Lane, '"When Blood is their Argument": class, character, and historymaking in Shakespeare's and Branagh's *Henry V*', *English Literary History*, 61 (1994), 27–52, at p. 46.
19. *Shakespeare on Film*, p. 124.
20. *Filming Shakespeare's Plays: The Adaptations of Laurence Olivier, Orson Welles, Peter Brook and Akira Kurosawa* (Cambridge: Cambridge University Press, 1988), p. 166.
21. Wheale, In Lesley Aers and Nigel Wheale, *Shakespeare in the Changing Curriculum* (London: Routledge, 1991), p. 6.
22. *Shakespeare, Cinema and Society*, p. 193.
23. *Shakespeare on Film*, p. 167.
24. Charles Marowitz, *Recycling Shakespeare* (London: Macmillan, 1991).

Further Reading

1 Shakespeare, Film and Violence: Doing Violence to Shakespeare

Barker, Francis. *The Culture of Violence: Tragedy and History.* Manchester: Manchester University Press, 1993.

Bate, Jonathan. 'Introduction', in Bate, ed. *Titus Andronicus.* London: Routledge, 1995, pp. 1–121.

Sales, Roger. 'The Theatre of Hell', in *Christopher Marlowe.* London: Macmillan, 1991, pp. 11–32.

Film Criticism

Bulman, J. C., and H. R. Coursen, eds. *Shakepeare on Television* (extracts from reviews of the Granada *Lear).* Hanover and London: University Press of New England, 1988, pp. 287–9, 299–303.

Holderness, Graham. 'Radical Potential: Macbeth on Film', in *Macbeth: A Casebook,* ed. Alan Sinfield. London: Macmillan, 1992, pp. 151–60.

Jorgens, Jack. 'Roman Polanski's Macbeth', in *Shakespeare on Film.* Bloomington: Indiana University Press, 1977, pp. 161–74.

Manvell, Roger. *Shakespeare and the Film.* London: Dent, 1971, pp. 133–52.

Pearlman, E. '*Macbeth* on Film: Politics', in *Shakespeare and the Moving Image: The Plays on Film and Television,* ed. Anthony Davies and Stanley Wells. Cambridge: Cambridge University Press, 1994, pp. 250–60.

Rothwell, Kenneth S. 'In Search of Nothing: Mapping *King Lear*', in *Shakespeare the Movie: Popularizing the Plays on Film, TV, and Video,* ed. Lynda E. Boose and Richard Burt. London and New York: Routledge, 1997, pp. 135–47.

Shaw, William P. 'Violence and vision in Polanski's *Macbeth* and Brook's *Lear*', *Literature/Film Quarterly,* 4:4 (1986), 211–13.

2   Shakespeare, Film and Gender: Critical and Filmic Respresentations of *Hamlet*

Film Criticism

Barnett, Mark Thornton. 'The "Very Cunning of the Scene": Kenneth Branagh's *Hamlet', Literature/Film Quarterly*, 25:2 (1997), 78–82.

Coursen, H. R. '"What's there?": Opening *Hamlet* on Film', in *Entering the Maze: Shakespeare's Art of Beginning*. New York: Peter Lang, 1995, pp. 95–120.

Davison, Peter. *Text in Performance: 'Hamlet'*. London: Macmillan, 1983, pp. 47–54.

Dawson, Anthony B. *Shakespeare in Performance: 'Hamlet'*. Manchester: Manchester University Press, 1995, pp. 170–223.

Hodgdon, Barbara. 'The Critic, the Poor Player, Prince Hamlet, and the Lady in the Dark', in *Shakespeare Reread: The Texts in New Contexts*, ed. Russ McDonald. Ithaca and London: Cornell University Press, 1994, pp. 259–94.

Klein, Holger and Dimiter Daphinoff, eds. *'Hamlet' on Screen, The Shakespeare Yearbook*, Vol. 8, Lewiston, NY: Edwin Mellen Press, 1997.

Kliman, Bernice. *'Hamlet': Film Television and Audio Performance*. London: Associated University Presses, 1988.

McComb, John P. 'Toward an Objective Correlative: The Problem of Desire in Franco Zeffirelli's *Hamlet', Literature/Film Quarterly*, 25:2 (1997), 125–32.

Simmons, James R. Jr.'"In the Rank Sweat of an Enseamed Bed": Sexual Aberration and the Paradigmatic Screen *Hamlets', Literature/Film Quarterly*, 25:2 (1997), 111–18.

Taylor, Neil. 'The films of *Hamlet'*, in *Shakespeare and the Moving Image: The Plays on Film and Television*, ed. A. Davies and S. Wells. Cambridge: Cambridge University Press, 1994, pp. 180–95.

Weller, Philip. 'Freud's Footprints in Films of *Hamlet', Literature/Film Quarterly*, 25:2 (1997), 119–24.

Welsh, Jim. 'Branagh's Enlarged *Hamlet', Literature/Film Quarterly*, 25:2 (1997), 154–5.

3   Shakespeare, Film and Sexuality: Politically Correct Sexuality in Film Adaptations of *Romeo and Juliet* and *Much Ado About Nothing*

Film Criticism

Branagh, Kenneth. *'Much Ado About Nothing': The Making of the Movie*. New York: Norton, 1993.

Davies, Anthony. 'The film versions of Romeo and Juliet', *Shakespeare Survey*, 49 (1996), 153–62.

Deats, Sara Manson. 'Zeffirelli's *Romeo and Juliet:* Shakespeare for the sixties', *Studies in Popular Culture*, 6 (1983), 60–7.

Donaldson, Peter S. *Shakespearean Films/Shakespearean Directors*. Boston and London: Unwin Hyman, 1990, pp. 145–88.

Edgerton, Ellen. '"Your answer, sir, is cinematical": Kenneth Branagh's *Much Ado About Nothing*', *Shakespeare Bulletin*, 12 (1994), 42–5.

Hapgood, Robert. 'The Artistry of Franco Zeffirelli', in *Shakespeare the Movie: Popularizing the Plays on Film, TV, and Video*, ed. Lynda E. Boose and Richard Burt. London and New York: Routledge, 1997.

Holmer, Joan Ozark. 'The poetics of paradox: Shakespeare's versus Zeffirelli's cultures of violence', *Shakespeare Survey*, 49 (1996), 163–80.

Jorgens, Jack. 'Franco Zeffirelli's *Romeo and Juliet*', in *Shakespeare on Film*. Bloomington and London: Indiana University Press, 1977, pp. 79–91.

Levenson, Jill. *Shakespeare in Performance: 'Romeo and Juliet'*. Manchester and New York: Manchester University Press, 1987, pp. 104–23.

Murray, Timothy. 'Introduction' to *Drama Trauma: Specters of Race and Sexuality in Performance, Video and Art*. London and New York: Routledge, 1997, pp. 1–28 (relevant to Baz Luhrmann's *William Shakespeare's Romeo + Juliet*).

Van Watson, William. 'Shakespeare, Zeffirelli, and the Homosexual Gaze', in *Shakespeare and Gender: A History*, ed. Deborah Barker and Ivo Kamps. London: Verso, 1995, pp. 235–62.

Welsh, Jim. 'Postmodern Shakespeare: Strictly *Romeo*', *Literature/Film Quarterly*, 25:2 (1997), 154–5.

4 Shakespeare, Film and Race: Screening *Othello* and *The Tempest*

Bartels, Emily. 'Making More of the Moor: Aaron, Othello and Renaissance Refashionings of Race', *Shakespeare Quarterly*, 41 (1990), 433–54.

Brown, Paul. '"This thing of darkness I acknowledge mine": *The Tempest* and the discourse of colonialism', in *Political Shakespeare*, ed. J. Dollimore and A. Sinfield, 1985; 2nd edn Manchester: Manchester University Press, 1994, pp. 48–71.

Callaghan, Dympna. '"Othello was a white man": properties of race on Shakespeare's stage', in *Alternative Shakespeares*, Vol. 2, ed. Terence Hawkes. London and New York: Routledge, 1996, pp. 192–215.

Hendricks, Margo and Patricia Parker, eds. *Women, 'Race', & Writing in the Early Modern Period.* New York and London: Routledge, 1994.

Little, Arthur L., Jr. '"An essence that's not seen": The Primal Scene of Racism in *Othello*', *Shakespeare Quarterly*, 3 (1993), 304–24.

Loomba, A. *Gender, Race, Renaissance Drama.* Manchester: Manchester University Press, 1989.

Neill, Michael. '"Unproper Beds": Race, Adultery and the Hideous in *Othello*', *Shakespeare Quarterly*, 40 (1989), 383–412.

Newman, K. '"And wash the Ethiop white": femininity and the monstrous in *Othello*', in *Shakespeare Reproduced: The Text in History and Ideology,* ed. Jean E. Howard and Marion F. O'Connor. New York and London: Routledge, 1987, pp. 141–62.

Salway, John. 'Veritable negroes and circumcized dogs: racial disturbances in Shakespeare', in *Shakespeare in the Changing Curriculum,* ed. L. Aers and N. Wheale. London and New York: Routledge, 1989, pp. 108–24.

Film Criticism

Cavecchi, Mariacritina. 'Peter Greenaway's *Prospero's Books*: A Tempest Between Word and Image', *Literature/Film Quarterly*, 25:2 (1997), 83–9.

Davies, Anthony. *Filming Shakespeare's Plays: The Adaptations of Laurence Olivier, Orson Welles, Peter Brook and Akira Kurosawa.* Cambridge: Cambridge University Press, 1988, pp. 100–18, 193–4.

Donaldson, Peter S. 'Shakespeare in the Age of Post-Mechanical

Reproduction: Sexual and Electronic Magic in *Prospero's Books'*, in *Shakespeare the Movie: Popularizing the Plays on Film, TV, and Video*, ed. Lynda E. Boose and Richard Burt. London and New York: Routledge, 1997, pp. 169–85.

Harris, Diana and Jackson MacDonald. 'Stormy Weather: Derek Jarman's *The Tempest'*, *Literature/Film Quarterly*, 25 (1997), 90–8.

Hodgdon, Barbara. 'Race-ing *Othello*, Re-Engendering White-Out', in *The Shakespeare Trade: Performances & Appropriations*. Philadelphia: University of Pennsylvania Press, 1998, pp. 39–73.

Jorgens, Jack J. *Shakespeare on Film*. Bloomington and London: Indiana University Press, 1977, pp. 175–90, 290–4, 325–6.

Lanier, Douglas. 'Drowning the Book: *Prospero's Books* and the Textual Shakespeare', 1996, rpt. *New Casebooks: Shakespeare on Film*, ed. Robert Shaughnessy. Basingstoke and London: Macmillan, 1998, pp. 173–95.

MacCabe, Colin. 'A Post-National European Cinema: A Consideration of Derek Jarman's *The Tempest* and *Edward II'*, 1992; rpt. *New Casebooks: Shakespeare on Film*, ed. Robert Shaughnessy. Basingstoke and London: Macmillan, 1998, pp. 145–55.

Murray, Timothy. 'Dirty Stills: Arcadian Retrospection, Cinematic Hieroglyphs, and Blackness Run Riot in Olivier's *Othello'*, in *Like a Film: Ideological Fantasy on Screen, Camera and Canvas*. London and New York: Routledge, 1993, pp. 101–23.

Washington, Paul. '"This Last Tempest": Shakespeare, Postmodernity and *Prospero's Books'*, in *Shakespeare: World Views*, ed. Heather Kerr, Robin Eaden and Madge Mitton. Newark and London: University of Delaware Press and Associated University Presses, 1996, pp. 237–48.

5   Shakespeare, Film and Nationalism: *Henry V*

Film Criticism

Breight, Curtis. 'Branagh and the Prince, or a "royal fellowship of death"' (1991), in *New Casebooks: Shakespeare on Film*, ed. Robert Shaughnessy. Basingstoke and London: Macmillan, 1998, pp. 126–44.

Collick, John. *Shakepeare, Cinema, and Society*. Manchester: Manchester University Press, 1989, pp. 47–51.

Crowl, Stanley. *Shakespeare Observed: Studies in Performance on Stage and Screen.* Cambridge: Cambridge University Press, 1993, pp. 165–74, 189–90.

Davies, Anthony. *Filming Shakespeare's Plays: The Adaptations of Laurence Olivier, Orson Welles, Peter Brook and Akira Kurosawa.* Cambridge: Cambridge University Press, 1988, pp. 26–37, 189–90.

Deats, S. 'Rabbits and ducks: Olivier, Branagh and *Henry V*', *Literature/Film Quarterly*, 20 (1992), 284–93.

Donaldson, Peter S. 'Taking on Shakespeare: Kenneth Branagh's *Henry V*', *Shakespeare Quarterly*, 42 (1991), 60–71.

Fitter, Chris, 'A Tale of Two Branagh's: *Henry V*, Ideology and the Makong Agincourt', in *Shakespeare Left and Right*, ed. Ivo Kamps. London: Routledge, 1991, pp. 259–76.

Geduld, Harry M. *Filmguide to 'Henry V'.* Bloomington and London: Indiana University Press, 1973.

Hedrick, Donald K. 'War is Mud: Branagh's Dirty Harry V and the Types of Political Ambiguity', in *Shakespeare the Movie: Popularizing the Plays on Film, TV, and Video*, ed. Lynda E. Boose and Richard Burt. New York and London: Routledge, 1997, pp. 45–66.

Holderness, Graham, 'Reproductions: *Henry V*', in *Shakespeare Recycled: The Making of Historical Drama.* New York and London: Harvester Wheatsheaf, 1992, pp. 178–210.

Howard, Jean E. and Phyllis Rackin. 'Thoroughly Modern Henry', in *Engendering a Nation: A Feminist Account of Shakespeare's English Histories.* London and New York: Routledge, 1997, pp. 3–10.

Jorgens, Jack J. *Shakespeare on Film.* Bloomington and London: Indiana University Press, 1977, pp. 122–35, 272–5, 321.

Lane, Robert. '"When blood is their argument": class, character and historymaking in Shakespeare's and Branagh's *Henry V*', *English Literary History*, 61 (1994), 27–52.

Bibliography

Aers, Lesley and Nigel Wheale. *Shakespeare in the Changing Curriculum*. London: Routledge, 1991.

Barker, Deborah and Ivo Kamps, eds. *Shakespeare and Gender: A History*. London: Verso, 1995.

Barker, Francis. *The Culture of Violence: Shakespeare, Tragedy, History*. Manchester: Manchester University Press, 1993.

Bayley, John. *Shakespeare and Tragedy*. London: Routledge & Kegan Paul, 1981.

Bennett, Susan. *Performing Nostalgia: Shifting Shakespeare and the Contemporary Past*. London: Routledge, 1996.

Boose, Lynda E. 'Scolding brides and bridling scolds: taming the woman's unruly member', *Shakespeare Quarterly*, 42 (1991), 171-213.

Boose, Lynda E. and Richard Burt, eds. *Shakespeare the Movie: Popularizing the Plays on Film, TV, and Video*. London and New York: Routledge, 1997.

Branagh, Kenneth. *Beginning*. New York: Norton, 1989.

Branagh, Kenneth. *'Much Ado About Nothing': The Making of the Movie*. New York: Norton, 1993.

Branagh, Kenneth. *'Hamlet' by William Shakespeare: Screenplay, Introduction and Film Diary*. London: Chatto & Windus, 1996.

Briggs, Julia. *This Stage-Play World: Texts and Contexts, 1580–1625*. 1983; 2nd edn Oxford and New York: Oxford University Press, 1997.

Buchman, Lorne M. *Still in Movement: Shakespeare on Screen*. New York and Oxford: Oxford University Press, 1991.

Bulman, James C. *Shakespeare, Theory, and Performance*. New York and London: Routledge, 1996.

Butcher, Philip. 'Othello's Racial Identity', *Shakespeare Quarterly*, 111 (1952), 243-9.

Chedgzoy, Kate. *Shakespeare's Queer Children: Sexual Politics and*

Contemporary Culture. Manchester: Manchester University Press, 1995.

Collick, John. *Shakespeare, Cinema and Society*. Manchester: Manchester University Press, 1989.

Conan, S. and I. R. Hark, eds. *Screening the Male*. London: Routledge, 1993.

Cookson, S. and Bryan Loughrey, eds. *Critical Essays on 'Much Ado About Nothing'*. New York: Longman, 1989.

Costello, T. *International Guide to Literature on Film*. London: Bowker-Saur, 1994.

Crowl, Stanley. *Shakespeare Observed: Studies in Performance on Stage and Screen*. Cambridge: Cambridge University Press, 1993.

Davies, Anthony. *Filming Shakespeare's Plays: The Adaptations of Laurence Olivier, Orson Welles, Peter Brook and Akira Kurosawa*. Cambridge: Cambridge University Press, 1988.

Davies, Anthony. 'The film versions of *Romeo and Juliet*', *Shakespeare Survey*, 49 (1996), 153–62.

Davies, Anthony and Stanley Wells, eds. *Shakespeare and the Moving Image: The Plays on Film and Television*. Cambridge: Cambridge University Press, 1994.

Davison, Peter. *'Hamlet': Text and Performance*. London: Macmillan, 1983.

Dawson, Anthony B. *Shakespeare in Performance: 'Hamlet'*. Manchester: Manchester University Press, 1995, pp. 170–223.

Deats, Sara Manson. 'Rabbits and ducks: Olivier, Branagh and *Henry V*', *Literature/Film Quarterly*, 20 (1992), 284-93.

Dessen, Alan. *'Titus Andronicus'*. Manchester: Manchester University Press, 1992.

Dollimore, Jonathan and Alan Sinfield, eds. *Political Shakespeare*. 1985; rpt. Manchester: Manchester University Press, 1994.

Donaldson, Peter S. *Shakespearean Films/Shakespearean Directors*. London and Boston: Unwin Hyman, 1990.

Drakakis, John, ed. *Alternative Shakespeares*. London: Methuen, 1985.

Dusinberre, Juliet. *Shakespeare and the Nature of Women*. London: Macmillan, 1975.

Eagleton, Terry. *William Shakespeare*. Oxford: Blackwell, 1986.

Eckert, Charles, ed. *Focus on Shakespearean Films*. Englewood Cliffs: Prentice Hall, 1972.

Edgerton, Ellen. '"Your answer, sir, is cinematical": Kenneth

Branagh's *Much Ado About Nothing',* *Shakespeare Bulletin,* 12 (1994), 42–5.

Fermor, Una Ellis. *The Frontiers of Drama.* London: Methuen, 1945.

Garber, Margarie. *Coming of Age in Shakespeare.* London and New York: Methuen, 1981.

Geduld, Harry M. *Filmguide to 'Henry V'.* Bloomington: Indiana University Press, 1973.

Grant, Cathy, ed. *As You Like It: Audio Visual Shakespeare,* London: British Universities Film & Video Council, 1992.

Greenblatt, Stephen. *Shakespearean Negotiations: The Circulation of Social Energy in Renaissance England.* Berkeley: University of California Press, 1988.

Hawkes, Terence. *Meaning by Shakespeare.* London and New York: Routledge, 1992.

Hawkes, Terence, ed. *Alternative Shakespeares,* Vol. 2. London and New York: Routledge, 1996.

Hawkins, Harriet. 'From *King Lear* to *King Kong* and Back: Shakespeare and Popular Modern Genres', in *Classics and Trash: Traditions and Taboos in High Literature and Popular Modern Genres.* London and New York: Harvester Wheatsheaf, 1990, pp. 103–38.

Hendricks, Margo and Patricia Parker, eds. *Women, 'Race', & Writing in the Early Modern Period.* New York and London: Routledge, 1994.

Higham, Charles. *The Films of Orson Welles.* Berkeley: University of California Press, 1970.

Holderness, Graham, ed. *The Shakespeare Myth.* Manchester: Manchester University Press, 1988.

Holderness, Graham, ed. *Shakespeare's History Plays.* New Casebooks. London: Macmillan, 1992.

Holderness, Graham. *Shakespeare Recycled: The Making of Historical Drama.* New York and London: Harvester Wheatsheaf, 1992.

Holmer, Joan Ozark. 'The poetics of paradox: Shakespeare's versus Zeffirelli's cultures of violence', *Shakespeare Survey,* 49 (1996), 163–80.

Howard, Jean E. and M. O'Connor. *Shakespeare Reproduced: The Text in History and Ideology.* London: Methuen, 1987.

Howard, Jean E. and Phyllis Rackin. *Engendering a Nation: A Feminist Account of Shakespeare's English Histories.* London and New York: Routledge, 1997.

Jardine, Lisa. *Still Harping on Daughters: Women and Drama in the Age of Shakespeare.* 1983; 2nd edn. New York, London and Toronto: Harvester, 1989.

Jardine, Lisa. *Reading Shakespeare Historically.* London and New York, 1996.

Jarman, Derek. *Dancing Ledge.* 1984; rpt. London: Quartet, 1991.

Jones, Ernest, '*Hamlet' and Oedipus,* 1949; rpt. New York: Norton, 1976.

Jorgens, Jack. *Shakespeare on Film.* Bloomington and London: Indiana University Press, 1977.

Joughin, John J., ed. *Shakespeare and National Culture.* Manchester and New York: Manchester University Press, 1997.

Jump, John, ed. *'Macbeth'.* London: Macmillan, 1968.

Kamps, Ivo, ed. *Shakespeare Left and Right.* London: Routledge, 1991.

Kerr, Heather, Robin Eaden and Madge Mitton, eds. *Shakespeare: World Views.* Newark and London: University of Delaware Press and Associated University Presses, 1996.

Klein, Holger and Dimiter Daphinoff, eds. *'Hamlet' on Screen, The Shakespeare Yearbook,* Vol. 8. Lewiston, NY: Edwin Mellen Press, 1997.

Kliman, Bernice W. *'Hamlet': Film, Television and Audio Performance.* London: Associated University Presses, 1988.

Kliman, Bernice W. *'Macbeth': Text and Performance.* London: Macmillan, 1992.

Knight, Wilson. *The Olive and the Sword.* Oxford: Oxford University Press, 1944.

Lane, Robert. '"When blood is their argument": class, character, and historymaking in Shakespeare's and Branagh's *Henry V', English Literary History,* 61 (1994), 27–52.

Lenz, C. R. S., G. Greene and C. Thomas, eds. *The Women's Part: Feminist Criticism of Shakespeare.* Champaign: University of Illinois Press, 1980.

Loomba, Ania, *Gender, Race and Renaissance Drama.* Manchester: Manchester University Press, 1989.

McDonald, Russ, ed. *Shakespeare Reread: The Texts in New Contexts.* Ithaca: Cornell University Press, 1994.

MacFarlane, Brian, *Novel to Film: An Introduction to the Theory of Adaptation.* Oxford: Clarendon, 1996.

McKernan, Luke and Olwen Terris, eds. *Walking Shadows: Shakespeare in the National Film and Television Archive.* London: National Film Theatre, 1994.

Manvell, Roger. *Shakespeare and the Film*. London: Dent, 1971.

Marowitz, Charles. *Recycling Shakespeare*. London: Macmillan, 1991.

Marsden, Jean I., ed. *The Appropriation of Shakespeare: Post-Renaissance Reconstructions of the Works and the Myth*. New York and London: Harvester Wheatsheaf, 1991.

Mast, G. and M. Cohen, eds. *Film Theory and Criticism*. Oxford: Oxford University Press, 1974.

Monaco, James, *How to Read a Film*. New York and Oxford: Oxford University Press, 1981.

Mulvey, Laura. 'Visual pleasure and narrative cinema', *Screen*, 16:3 (1975), 6–19.

Murray, Timothy. 'Dirty Stills: Arcadian Retrospection, Cinematic Hieroglyphs, and Blackness Run Riot in Olivier's *Othello*', in *Like a Film: Ideological Fantasy on Screen, Camera and Canvas*. London and New York: Routledge, 1993, pp. 101–23.

Murray, Timothy. *Drama Trauma: Specters of Race and Sexuality in Performance, Video and Art*. London and New York: Routledge, 1997.

Olivier, Laurence. *Confessions of an Actor: An Autobiography*. New York: Weidenfeld & Nicolson, 1982.

Olivier, Laurence. *On Acting*. London: Weidenfeld & Nicolson, 1986.

Palmer, D. J. 'The unspeakable in pursuit of the uneatable: language and action in *Titus Andronicus*', *Critical Quarterly*, 14 (1972), 320–39.

Partridge, Eric. *Shakespeare's Bawdy*. 1947; 3rd edn. rpt. London and New York: Routledge, 1990.

Pribram, E. Deidre, ed. *Female Spectators*. London: Verso, 1988.

Rothwell, K. and Annabel Henkin Melza, eds. *Shakespeare on Screen: An International Filmography and Videography*. London, Mansell, 1990.

Sales, Roger. *Christopher Marlowe*. London: Macmillan, 1991.

Shaughnessy, Robert, ed. *New Casebooks: Shakespeare on Film*. Basingstoke and London: Macmillan, 1998.

Shaw, William P. 'Violence and vision in Polanski's *Macbeth* and Brook's *Lear*', *Literature/Film Quarterly*, 4:4 (1986), 211–13.

Silviria, Dale. *Laurence Olivier and the Art of Film Making*. Rutherford: Fairleigh Dickenson University Press, 1985.

Sinfield, Alan, ed. *'Macbeth': Contemporary Critical Essays*. London: Macmillan, 1992.

Sinyard, Neil. *Filming Literature*. London: Croom Helm, 1986.

Smith, Peter J. *Social Shakespeare*. London: Macmillan, 1995.

Spurgeon, Caroline. *Shakespeare's Imagery and What it Tells Us*. 1935; rpt. Cambridge: Cambridge University Press, 1993.

Tillyard, E. M. W. *Shakespeare's History Plays*, 1944; rpt. London: Chatto & Windus, 1964.

Traub, Valerie. *Desire and Anxiety: Circulations of Sexuality in Shakespearean Drama*. London: Routledge, 1992.

Van Doren, Mark. *Shakespeare*. 1939; rpt. Garden City: Doubleday, 1953.

Watts, Cedric. *'Romeo and Juliet'*. (Harvester New Critical Introductions to Shakespeare). Brighton: Harvester, 1991.

Willson, Robert F., ed. *Entering the Maze: Shakespeare's Art of Beginning*. New York: Peter Lang, 1995.

Wilson, Richard. *Will Power: Essays on Shakespearean Authority*. New York and London: Harvester Wheatsheaf, 1993.

Wofford, Susanne L. *'Hamlet': Case Studies in Contemporary Criticism*. Boston and New York: St Martin's Press and Macmillan, 1994.

Filmography of Major Films Discussed

1   Shakespeare, Film and Violence: Doing Violence to Shakespeare

Theatre of Blood (1973), directed by Douglas Hickox, starring Vincent Price (UK)

King Lear (1971), directed by Peter Brook, starring Paul Scofield (UK/Denmark)

King Lear (1982), directed by Jonathan Miller (BBC), starring Michael Hordern (UK/USA)

King Lear (1983), directed by Michael Elliot (ITV), starring Laurence Olivier (UK)

King Lear (1997), directed by Richard Eyre (BBC), starring Ian Holm (UK)

Macbeth (1971), directed by Roman Polanski, starring Jon Finch (UK)

2   Shakespeare, Film and Gender: Critical and Filmic Respresentations of *Hamlet*

Hamlet (1948), directed by Laurence Olivier, starring Laurence Olivier (UK)

Hamlet (1964), directed by G. Kosintsev, starring I. Smukhtunovski (USSR)

Hamlet (1969), directed by Tony Richardson, starring Nicol Williamson (UK)

Hamlet (1980), directed by Rodney Bennett (BBC), starring Derek Jacobi (UK/USA)

Hamlet (1990), directed by Franco Zeffirelli, starring Mel Gibson (UK/France/Spain)

Hamlet (1996), directed by Kenneth Branagh, starring Kenneth Branagh (UK/USA)

3   Shakespeare, Film and Sexuality: Politically Correct Sexuality in Film Adaptations of *Romeo and Juliet* and *Much Ado About Nothing*

Romeo and Juliet (1968), directed by Franco Zeffirelli, starring Olivia Hussey and Leonard Whiting (UK/Italy)
William Shakespeare's Romeo + Juliet (1996), directed by Baz Luhrmann, starring Leonardo Di Caprio and Claire Danes (USA)
Much Ado About Nothing (1993), directed by Kenneth Branagh, starring Kenneth Branagh and Emma Thompson

4   Shakespeare, Film and Race: Screening *Othello* and *The Tempest*

The Tragedy of Othello: The Moor of Venice (1952), directed by Orson Welles, starring Orson Welles (USA/Italy/France/Morocco)
Othello (1965), directed by Stuart Burge, starring Laurence Olivier (UK)
Othello (1995), directed by Oliver Parker, starring Laurence Fishburne (USA/UK)
The Tempest (1979), directed by Derek Jarman, starring Heathcote Williams (UK)
The Tempest (1980), directed by John Gorrie (BBC), starring Michael Hordern (UK/USA)
Prospero's Books (1991), directed by Peter Greenaway, starring John Gielgud (France/Italy/Netherlands/UK)

5   Shakespeare, Film and Nationalism: *Henry V*

Henry V (1944), directed by Laurence Olivier, starring Laurence Olivier (UK/USA)
Henry V (1989), directed by Kenneth Branagh, starring Kenneth Branagh (UK/ USA)

6 Conclusions

In the Bleak Midwinter (UK), *A Midwinter's Tale* (USA) (1995), directed by Kenneth Branagh, starring Michael Maloney (UK/USA)
Looking for Richard (1996), directed by Al Pacino, starring Al Pacino (USA)
Shakespeare in Love (1998), directed by John Madden, starring Joseph Fiennes and Gwyneth Paltrow (USA/UK)

Index